F
Voice
in a time of crisis

ISBN 978-1-80049-889-1
First Edition

Printed and bound in Great Britain by Clays Ltd,
Elcograf S.p.A

Thank you to the NHS staff who have written accounts. They are not simply reflections on Covid-19 amassed after the fact, but instead are stories which have been relayed in the moment - in phone calls made after long shifts on respiratory wards or via emails sent late at night by exhausted doctors too terrified to kiss their own children goodnight.

PREFACE

Robert Crampton
The Times columnist.
March 2020

When did you first realise this was going to be serious? Or actually, not just serious, serious does not nearly do the last 12 months justice. Neither do "major" or "massive". How about we bring in "epochal" and settle on that? Epochal as in something that happens once or twice every century, and then defines that century. Like the first and second world wars did in the last century.

So, when did you initially clock that the pandemic that has ruled our lives and our conversation for a year was an epochal event? When the first cases started to be reported out of Wuhan last January? When the first UK victim was identified in February? When the first lockdown was imposed last March? Or last April, when the deaths started to multiply? Or in the summer, when it annoyingly failed fully to go away, as most of us (despite what the experts said) secretly and yet confidently assumed it would? Or did it take you until early December, when Christmas got binned?

My own feeling is that realisation of the historical significance of Covid 19 has not come in any one particular lightbulb moment, as it did when JFK got shot or the Twin Towers came down, but has rather been a gradual dawning process that we're living and dying through something extraordinary. I think that process is still ongoing. That even now, one year in, we haven't truly begun to appreciate the scale of what has happened.

While a slow gradual assessment might, however, sound familiar to most of us, the NHS workers whose stories are told in the following pages had no such luxury. They knew this was an absolute top grade emergency straight off, from last February onwards, when surgeries and wards and ICUs started to fill with scores and then hundreds and then thousands of desperately ill people struggling to breathe. For frontline workers, give or take a brief respite last summer, the battle to help those stricken patients keep breathing has gone on ever since.

Even as the crisis eases, even as details of the brutally heart-rending nature of the struggle begin to emerge in accounts such as those following, it will be many years before the rest of us fully appreciate the full extent of the sacrifices made.

The comparison to the wars of the last century is justified. It was all going to be over by Christmas. There was a period of phoney war when nothing awful happened. And then, when plenty of awful things happened all at once, mistakes ensued. And there was no end in sight. And on it went. And then, deliverance was at hand. But still it took forever. And even when it was over, it wasn't quite, because now as in 1918 and 1945, in 2021 we'll be living with the consequences for a long time.

In some respects, this modern conflict has been even tougher than the nation's previous titanic struggle of 1939-45. Then, we had a clearly identifiable conspicuously evil enemy. Now, it makes no sense to call an insensate microscopic virus "evil". It's hard to whip up a sense of solidarity against a microcosm. Then, the victims of the conflagration and the damage it inflicted were all too visible. Now, the terrible toll lacks a human face, thousands of individual tragedies reduced to statistics in a chart in the newspapers. When the dust settles and normality resumes, the sheer loneliness in their final days of those who succumbed will surely constitute the greatest tragedy. A loneliness only alleviated by the extraordinary human kindness demonstrated by those medics who risked their own lives to offer comfort as the end neared.

If you read accounts of those who served in the second world war, as soldiers or sailors, airmen or air raid wardens, nurses or Normandy veterans, those accounts tend to have one thing in common: what we did, they say, wasn't anything special. No big deal. It is instructive that many of the interviewees in the following pages are similarly modest. True heroes seem to have a habit of downplaying, even denying, their own courage. They feel themselves part of a bigger collective effort. And so they are. They are also acutely aware of the colleagues and comrades who, equally brave though they were, were not lucky enough to survive.

What is the classic image of a hero of the second world war? A handsome devil-may-care impossibly young man with a pencil moustache in the cockpit of a Spitfire,? A grim-faced Tommy doing his duty in the desert? A lantern-jawed Royal Navy officer in a chunky roll-neck sweater on the bridge of a destroyer in the freezing north Atlantic? Heroes all, for sure. And also, all male, all white, all under the age of 30, all born within the borders of the United Kingdom.

The heroes of the present struggle are vastly different. Many are middle aged. Many were not born in Britain. Many do not have a white skin. And many - indeed a majority - are women. When, back in April and May last year, I joined my family outside our front door clapping for carers, the composite image I had in mind of the person I was applauding was a middle-aged black woman, quite possibly born far from these shores. That image did not spring from nowhere. It came as a natural result of long experience of the NHS. Perhaps, if anything good is to come out of the calamity of 2020-2021, it will be an appreciation, not before time, that British citizens of all backgrounds deserve to take an honoured place in their country's history.

Rather like the youngsters back in 1940, these contemporary heroes were pitched into battle, against an implacable enemy, with shoddy equipment and muddled leadership. The onslaught had been predicted for ages, yet the funds and preparations were not in place. As we know, and as the forthcoming accounts confirm, front line combatants against Covid last spring had little or none of what they needed either to best perform their duties or to protect themselves from personal disaster. Supplies of protective gear were absent or inadequate. Nurses had to make do with home-made masks. Some resorted to using bin bags in lieu of gowns and scrubs. Some were advised to hold their breath. Eager schoolchildren were pressed into service hacking up old curtains and sheets for their mums to sew up as scrubs.

Policy was equally make do and mend. The first lockdown was not imposed for two weeks after it became blindingly obvious that it had to happen, not just sooner rather than later, but now. In the interim, the Cheltenham race festival plus major international football and rugby matches were allowed to convene. The prime minister went around shaking hands with all and sundry. Flights not only from China, but also Italy and Spain, already identified as virus hotspots, continued as usual. Scandalously, thousands of elderly hospital patients were returned to care homes, where many spread the virus to devastating and deathly effect. Places of what ought to have been relative safety became plague pits. Care home workers were afforded even less personal protection than were their peers in the NHS.

Throughout those early weeks, and ever since, and still, and correctly, the ebb and flow of advice and rules and regulations and laws regarding lockdown and restrictions has been governed by the overriding need for the NHS not to be overwhelmed by the virus. That one concern - of patients dying in corridors for want of beds, ventilators, oxygen, as happened in northern Italy in April - has governed every decision. And fair enough. We all recognised the necessity to manage the pandemic in this way, that delaying the flow of victims was the best way to minimise morbidity.

But consider this: there is more than one way to overwhelm the NHS. A surplus of sufferers is one;

a shortage of staff is another. If enough health workers had decided, back in April or more recently this winter, that the risks were simply too great for them to continue to go to work, as well they might, had they been lesser characters, the system would have been swamped from the other side of the equation. And yet they didn't down tools. Far from it. Retired workers returned to the payroll. Existing workers volunteered for double shifts. Poorly paid porters and receptionists stayed at their posts.

Either a year ago, when it was obvious they were insufficiently protected, and their colleagues were falling ill and in some cases dying, or two months ago when the initial clap for carers drama had long worn off and they were exhausted after months of grinding work, it would not have been unreasonable for those in the frontline to ease off. Pull the odd sickie. Stay at home under the duvet once in a while. Go back to where they were born.

But they didn't. They haven't. They stuck with it. Turned up. Day after day, night after night. Kept on keeping on. Therein lies their true heroism. It's been a sensational effort.

The full story has yet to be told. What follows is, in a modest way, a start.

INDEX

INDEX

25
Larisa Korda
Obstetrician. Volunteered to work in ICU.

35
John McKenna
Consultant anaesthetist.

39
Anonymous
ICU registrar.

49
Chelsie Mason
Paramedic.

53
Zoe Garstang
Speech therapist.

59
David Oliver
Consultant physician in geriatric and acute general internal medicine.

67
Daniel Brooke
Sports & exercise medicine registrar.
Redeployed to A&E.

71
Katie Ward
Consultant in respiratory and general medicine.
Seconded to the Nightingale Hospital.

79
Jann Tipping
Acute care nurse.

85
Adrienn Gyori
Junior doctor.

99
Ed Jabbari
Clinical research training fellow in the
Department of Clinical and Movement
Neurosciences. Volunteered to Covid ward.

103
Neil Greenberg, Derek Tracy & Mark Tarn
Occupational psychologists. Led the Mental Health staff support strategy at London Nightingale Hospital.

111
Waleed Fawzi
Consultant geriatric psychiatrist.

117
William Rickitts
Consultant chest physician.

125
Mhairi McKittrick
GP.

131
Alan Salama
Professor of nephrology.

141
Lisa Linpower
Junior doctor.

147
Sarah Ryan
Doctor.

153
Sarah Gotke
Specialist respiratory physiotherapist.

165
Eliana Shekarchi-Khanghahi
Senior house officer. Redeployed to the Covid High Dependency Unit.

173
Paul Bolton
Lead nurse for infection prevention & control.

179
Paul Hicks
Cleaner.

183
Kirstie Hill
Intensive care nurse.

189
Anonymous
Consultant chest physician.

195
Zudin Puthucheary
Intensive care consultant.
May 2020

203
Susan Michie
Professor of behavioural psychology, and member of the Scientific Advisory Group for Emergencies (SAGE).

VOICES

When you take your first step into the red zone something happens that transforms your fear into a sense of purpose and intent. You don't focus on the danger, but instead on what you're going to do to help.

Larisa Korda
Obstetrician. Volunteered to work in ICU.
June 2020

Looking back over the last few months of the Covid pandemic, it all feels so surreal. I'm not sure how long an average person may need to process all the events, the scenarios, the death, the triumphs and the mental assault of being part of the red zone, but I'm not there yet and I suspect some of it will involve a lifetime of realisation and reflection. One thing is for sure, life and my perspective on it will never be the same again.

When I made the decision to volunteer and told my mum, she wouldn't stop crying. Her fear over whether I was going to be protected and safe was overwhelming and, I have no doubt, triggered by my parents' experience of war in Yugoslavia. But it was also the reason I felt compelled to help in whatever capacity I could, knowing that I wanted to look back one day and feel that I played my part.

When you take your first step into the red zone something happens that transforms your fear into a sense of purpose and intent, and you end up leaving it behind at the door as the camaraderie and motivation to get the job done rallies you on. You don't focus on the danger, but instead on what you're going to do to help, which is just as well, because I imagine this must be how a soldier feels when they show up for battle. There is no possible option to turn away because just by showing up, you're already deeply involved and, inevitably, attached to the outcome of every single one of your patients.

My first day in the intensive care unit was actually on World Health Day. How ironic that on a day we were supposed to be celebrating the achievements of modern medicine, I found myself in the centre of one of the Covid wards, every single bed full, every single patient on multiple modes of life support, with medical staff running between each bed, in desperate attempts to save people from a virus we had no understanding of and had never seen before.

The scene I saw arriving there is one I will never forget. It was the literal equivalent of the frontline of a war zone, the sounds, the smells and the fear of death. The new armour of face visor, gown and mask, making people almost unrecognisable and difficult to hear above the sound of the machines and general din.

But in amongst it all was also a prevailing sense of pride. All my teaching and training as a doctor had served to prepare me for this. Never in a million years could I ever have imagined that on the day I took my Hippocratic Oath, I would be putting my own life on the line, with my colleagues, to save people from the clutches of a global pandemic.

Despite the desperation, the exhaustion I could see on the doctors and nurses faces, and the frustration of being without a cure, there were glimmers of hope even at the beginning and examples of outstanding humanity that made me realise how much I wanted to be a part of it all.

I remember the first ICU consultant I worked with. As we went round the ward, processing information about each patient, he asked what a particular comatose patient's occupation was. Someone shouted "musician" from across the bay and on his order, we turned on the radio and the music started. The first song was "How to Save a Life" by The Fray. It couldn't have been more poignant. We did it in the hope that the subconscious part of the patient, as he lay in a coma on his bed, normally a fit, young man, would respond and begin to heal.

Human consciousness is a difficult thing to explain. Medicine sees it as the difference between being alert and orientated or not, but there is far more to it that is spiritual and exists even when a person is in a coma. As humans, we are made up of dynamic fields of energy and vibration, interconnecting our mind, body and soul. According to quantum physics, at the subatomic level, matter and energy are both interchangeable. It has been said that matter is the densest form of spirit and spirit the lightest form of matter, meaning that the body can really be interpreted as the outward manifestation of the mind. If we can affect the mind through external cues, then surely we can influence recovery and the impact on the body.

I was fortunate to have been under the leadership of a fabulous holistically-minded anaesthetic consultant who also saw the benefits and importance of actions that the subconscious mind was capable of processing. So, each day, going round my patients, I would hold their hand, stroke their head and chat to them about what was happening. I could see all the nurses doing this too, as they held vigil over each patient's bed for twelve hours each, under the heat of the PPE they had to wear, but who still continued to wash each patient, wipe the excrement, and apply cream to their hands and pressure sores. They treated each individual with love, as if they were their own relative. Every single patient was important and everyone was given the absolute best chance of living. We realised that in the absence of relatives, we had to be their family, rooting for them and sharing video clips and FaceTime with their loved ones at home, just so they could still feel a part of a situation that they had no control over, putting all their faith in us as medics, and entrusting their loved one's lives in our hands.

Those responsibilities were never lost on me. I realised that people needed answers, to be told the truth of what was going on and most of all, to be given hope. I tried to provide all of this as authentically as I could, whilst also sharing my own personal diary of emotions and feelings that I experienced each day. These ranged anywhere between exhilaration and celebration at seeing someone recover, to anger and frustration at the injustice of lives that were being claimed by the destructive virus.

Despite the sadness, there were times of immense happiness and even laughter. To see a man whose young son had sent us a banner and cupcakes earlier in the day, stand up from his bed for the first time after being in a coma for five weeks, the entire ward erupted into cheers and applause. To get to hear the voice for the first time of a woman who, against all the odds, made it out and got to clutch the Easter egg I had saved for her and remembered that at her most ill, she recalled me promising to deliver her baby despite the fact she was 70! These are the magical moments I will remember forever. And then there are the stories and the legacies which I will carry, because the ones living them are no longer with us.

There was a man who was a cleaner in a local supermarket and contracted Covid that damaged his lungs irreparably, to a point that no method of ventilation or medication was able to rescue him. As we grappled with the agonising decision of whether to turn off his life support, we allowed his relatives to come and visit and get a chance to be with him. No one could bring themselves to decide on the inevitable. I came to see him on my day off. I wanted to say my goodbyes as I braced myself for the end. And that evening, he made the decision for us, his heart gave up when he arrested.

There was also a man who I got to see out of his coma. I remember his gentleness and compassion, as well as his temper and frustration at not being able to go home, as he fought with the inevitable delirium that came after being weaned off life support. Just as he was getting better, he suddenly took a turn for the worse and after an hour of relentless chest compressions, I will never forget the image of him lifeless against the sheets. The male nurse, tears running down his face, brought in the man's photos and favourite music, as I went to see his relatives who'd been called in. The tears and the emotion that came over me then was one of the darkest days of the crisis.

In truth, I haven't yet processed all those tears. There's no manual for telling you how to cope. The recovery for us healthcare workers is gradual and will require a lot of patience and time. There is something about training to save lives at all costs and suddenly not being able to that makes you feel impotent, helpless and limited, something that no medic is ever comfortable feeling. It scares us all that, despite all our training, we do not make the call between who lives and who dies. We do what we can to preserve human life in the form that we recognise but when that isn't enough, how do we move on?

For me, one of the biggest learning points from this pandemic has been about the value of life. My normal job involves bringing new life into the world, and this other extreme of losing lives shook me to the core. But, it made me realise just how precious life is and how it can be removed from us at any given time. One of my patient's wrote me a note when she was able to. It said: "Life is precious, it's a gift." Just stop and consider that for a moment. To come face to face with death and to feel powerless is the most terrifying moment of your life but also the greatest wake up call to start living your life to the full.

As one survivor, who had been on both heart and lung support put it, with tears streaming down his face, "I will never live my life the same way again." For those who survived Covid, their lives will never be the same. They will make sure of it. But for the rest of us, we too have a chance to live our lives differently.

The question is, will we take that chance and start living our lives how we would want to if we knew our days were numbered?

Dealing with a dying patient while wearing PPE felt like that bit in E.T. when E.T. is dying and all the people in suits come to get him.

John McKenna
Consultant anaesthetist.
May 2020

PPE is sweaty, it's painful, weirdly it feels like I'm underwater. You can feel your breathing and hear your breath, and it slows everything down. You can't easily go to the loo or have anything to eat or drink, a little break, all those small things that you do normally to make work easier. If I'm doing an all day operation, I can't just pop out of theatre for a cup of tea or I'll burn through PPE. We have to shower four or five times a day, and it takes 15 minutes to put the gear on each time. We're doing stuff in shifts, instead, and it's much more tiring.

It also makes my manual dexterity a disaster. For example, I put wires into people's jugulars all the time, it's not a problem. But one of the first ones that I had to do with three sets of gloves on, I dropped the wire because I couldn't feel it. My manual dexterity is really important and it's gone. Also we're not doing normal operations as frequently, so all of us in anaesthetics are rusty. I'm sure the surgeons are rusty as well.

I'm not an emotional person but one of the things that caught me off guard was dealing with a dying patient while wearing PPE. I felt, suddenly, like I was in that bit in E.T. when E.T. is dying, and all the people in suits come to get him. I was one of them. Regardless of where you go in the world you know if somebody is being kind to you, or somebody is angry by the tone of voice and facial expressions. That's universal. But at the moment, with patients, you come in in all your spaceman gear, and you don't really have that much of a human interaction. It's very difficult. And then you send a patient off to sleep.

I've never forgotten that as an anaesthetist you are frequently the last person a patient will ever speak to. You try to make someone comfortable and at ease, to make their possible last moments as pleasant as possible. I'm just this anonymous spaceman that has put this patient into a coma, and I don't know if they are going to survive. Is the last thing they see some random person that they can't have any connection with because they can't read facial expressions? I didn't really appreciate that facial expressions were such a big deal until you don't have them. They have been stripped away, and I'm not the only one struggling with it.

The hardest part is knowing you are not able to give the best care possible to each patient. You're not neglecting them, but trying to do the best for as many as possible.

Anonymous
ICU registrar.
May 2020

There was always a sense of foreboding with coronavirus in the news, spreading to Iran and Italy so violently. It started to hit home when all our operating lists were cancelled and each day we'd show up for work and have to be allocated training or roles while waiting for the pandemic to start on our doorstep.

We had to clear out our ICUs to create bed spaces for Covid-19 patients, while undergoing PPE fit testing to ensure that our face masks had no critical leaks as we would be doing aerosol generating procedures in the airway of infected patients. We were practising donning and doffing training for PPE, and running intubation drills.

It was these drills that hammered home the surrealness of the situation, discussions of having to intubate patients every 30 minutes or so. There were about 20 of us anaesthetists and operating department practitioners (OPDs) gathered in an empty theatre to run through drills, the tension pierced only by the typical dark humour that we deploy as a head-in-the-sand method.

The anticipation grew with discussions about crisis management, and how our hospital had emergency plans to be able to house up to 500 ventilated patients. We have the largest ICU in Europe and rarely break 50 ventilated patients spread over four units.

We have the importance of documenting events and discussions with patients drilled into us. But while the pandemic was at its peak, with two ventilated patients in each bed space and one nurse looking after three or more patients - standard ICU care for a ventilated patient is 1:1 ratio - the patients would deteriorate so rapidly, so severely and so often that there was never time to document between each one. We were being called from emergency to emergency, only able to put out fires before the next one.

Being anaesthetic trained means you're airway trained so although we had scores of doctors drafted in from other specialties, there are only a handful of us at any one time that are able to deal with these emergencies. On more than one occasion I was with a patient attempting to stabilise them when asked by my senior house officer, my junior, to help with another patient, my only answer being "if their oxygen sats are lower than these I'll come" and getting a fairly meek shake of the head in response.

The hardest part of working through this crisis is the difficulty in knowing you cannot give the best care possible to each patient. It took a while to make that mental shift, that you're not neglecting patients but doing the best for as many as possible. In the early days that was a really hard position to square away, emotionally and ethically. But as hard as it was for me personally I know it was infinitely harder for our ICU nurses as they are used to giving 1:1 patient care. I saw a few nurses breakdown in tears or lose their tempers over trivial things because of their inability to give the care they wanted to their patients.

There are patients that stick in your memory. Often after particular deaths or arrest calls we debrief as a team, but there hasn't been the option during the pandemic to take 20 minutes to discuss and reflect. I know many of the juniors were particularly shaken by a couple of patients, including a girl in her early 30s who had just given birth to her second child but never made it out of ICU. I tried reaching out to many of them via text or phone, but it's difficult, and with lockdown there's no option to meet outside of work. The best you can do is briefly wrap an arm around them before an overzealous manager or matron admonishes you for not social distancing...

My hardest test came with an Eastern European patient. During this pandemic as we were in ICU surrounded by infected patients there was a strict no visitor rule unless a patient was end of life, then it was one visitor, in PPE, for 15 mins, who then had to go straight home and self isolate for two weeks.

Our hospital had set up a "family liaison team" consisting of medical students under the guidance of retired ICU consultants who would comb through the electronic notes each day and phone the next of kin and update them, an essential task given our workload meant we were unable to routinely call families to update them.

This would, however, on occasion lead to relatives not realising how unwell their loved ones were, and taking the long ICU stays as a positive sign (it rarely is).

We had a gentleman, 42 years old, who had been on our unit for three weeks with single organ respiratory failure, who had not been improving. His lungs were becoming gradually stiffer and more difficult to oxygenate. He slowly and gradually got worse to the point where we were struggling to maintain his blood oxygen levels despite giving him 100 per cent oxygen.

I had to phone his wife via a translation service. I warned the translator before we started that it was a bad news situation and that it would be a difficult discussion. Breaking bad news and changing relatives' expectations is hard in person. It is harder by phone, and a thankless task via translator when robbed of any means of using body language or tone or reading the recipient's body language and tone.

I made my introductions, asked what she knew was happening at the moment. She was under the impression that her husband was doing well and that God was looking after him. Slowly I had to reel back her understanding of his disease. She was distraught, which is to be expected.

What blindsided me was her revelation that she was pregnant with his baby, and had no relatives or support in this country aside from her eight-year-old daughter. She became so distressed that the child took the phone, and the translator asked me to talk to her because she spoke some english. It was a task that took all my mental and emotional reserve, explaining I was looking after her dad and that he was very poorly.

After I hung up one of the nurses came to ask me a fairly routine question which I answered, and then my consultant appeared to ask me something else, only to stop and ask if I was ok... I nodded my head and as I got to the "e" in "yeah" my head was shaking and I broke down crying in full PPE. My consultant tried to hug me, talk to me, actively bat my hands away from rubbing my eyes and pinching the bridge of my nose to stop crying.

We were pretty quickly called to a patient's bedside though, which snaps your focus back.

I have seen two nurses unable to complete their shifts due to emotional distress, I have heard stories of more, one walking off mid-shift without telling anyone as she was clearly in such a state. She was found by security in the car park crying in her car.

As medics we've always revelled in the outrageous and the absurd: the patient with the butternut squash firmly stuck in an orifice that it has no business being in. The feats of dazzling stupidity rendering patients prostrated on an A&E trolley. The indestructibles on elephant-sized doses of recreational uppers/downers/mind warpers, lovingly cuddling an inflated latex glove with an inked smiley face, forged by a fed-up sister put in charge of babysitting Barnet's answer to Keith Richards.

With the Covid-19 pandemic there has been none of that. It's been heartbreak after heartbreak. Loss after loss. This is why you see the ward teams applauding patients as they leave the hospital, or cheering on their first faltering steps with the physios after a month on a ventilator. The victories have been few and far between.

Without the absurdity of the human condition giving us our moments of dark humour we've often struggled and been forced to face head-on the emotional difficulties encountered in our roles, leaving us clutching on to these individual positive rays of light as a psychological life raft.

Dealing with this aspect of our jobs is something I can't say I have ever been trained to do in my 12 years of studying and practising to date, with many still believing in emotional fortitude being an inherent trait and key to career success.

It's only in the last year have I heard the phrase "it's OK to not be OK" uttered within our profession, and I'm genuinely fearful that when it comes to healthcare workers many, if not most, are not OK.

Once I started seeing young, fit and healthy patients deteriorate because of Covid, that was when I realised it was paramount to take the pandemic seriously.

Chelsie Mason
Paramedic.
June 2020

I only truly realised the severity of the situation when I returned from a month off work. The work I had become accustomed to had changed significantly. Suddenly we were required to wear PPE for every patient and the hospitals had to adapt to the influx of Covid cases. We became flooded with calls from patients displaying Covid symptoms, ranging from the mild to the critical. Once I started seeing young, fit and healthy patients deteriorate because of Covid, that was when I realised it was paramount to take the pandemic seriously.

People are afraid to call the emergency services because they do not want to go into hospital knowing that there are Covid patients present. Though we are less busy than prior to the pandemic, the severity of symptoms in cases has risen.

Then I was diagnosed with Covid. I was shocked, I did not expect to be found positive while being completely asymptomatic. There was a feeling of guilt towards colleagues and patients I had been into contact with while not knowing about it. Initially, I did not want to tell my family, because I knew they would worry, and in the back of my mind I was fearful at the prospect that I could start developing symptoms.

Thankfully with the PPE I have at work I remain content with my safety. I am now required to wear an apron, gloves, and a mask for every patient I see. After each patient, the ambulance and all the equipment has to be rigorously cleaned and wiped down. But my fear does surface when I consider my family and friends, some of whom have pre-existing medical conditions.

As a key worker the pandemic has brought its own set of challenges. I lived with my parents but had to make the difficult decision to move out to ensure that they were as safe as possible. I could not risk knowing that I could be the one that passed Covid onto them. I was lucky enough to be able to move in with my partner who is also a key worker. If I ended up in a situation where I had been forced to live alone during this time I fear that my mental health would not have fared well. Being called by my grandparents asking me when I would be able to come and see them and being unable to give them an answer was one of the hardest things I have had to personally deal with.

We are being faced with things that we've never seen before. All I want to do is provide the best service I can, but the frustration I can't do that makes me cry.

Zoe Garstang
Speech therapist.
July 2020

Hospital has always been my normality. It is where I work, how I function and where I feel purpose. I am the clinical lead in my field and know my role so well, but Covid presented me with challenges and complexities that I've never experienced before. Patients were often intubated and ventilated so couldn't talk. They have a tube put through their nose and throat so how they communicate changes. If they survive, they have little strength, and the tracheostomy tube can often cause them damage. They also struggle to walk because their muscles are so weak. When a patient comes off a ventilator, they feel so confused. They are delirious. That can be the result of an infection or the side effects of the sedation. They can be aggressive in that delirium. We needed to work out if they'd had long term cognitive damage or if they'd had a stroke, or if they'd had a brain injury or if it was just persistent delirium. It was very difficult. We found it so incredibly hard. There were so many more patients to deal with, yet fewer therapists to treat them properly, because they'd been redeployed. If we'd had better staffing levels we could have optimised the quality of life for patients more. It was frustrating.

Covid isn't just about death or survival. I don't think the public realises that. It also causes disabilities. We know there is a really high chance of a stroke with Covid. There are some patients that I don't believe will ever be able to live alone again, get out of bed themselves again. They can need three people to assist them because they are so physically and cognitively impaired. There are others who now need dialysis three times a week, some who are now in end stage renal failure. In some cases, where there has been a history of mental health issues, it has triggered a relapse. We are just not sure what Covid does an individual.

Some of my colleagues were redeployed into a service called Lifelines, which was set up to bridge the gap between patients and their families. They facilitated the video calls and were there when a patient passed away. It was a traumatic job. That role has never existed before, and it tended to be young nurses doing the role. How do you deal with that in your early 20s when you're just starting out in the profession? To process what we've seen, you have to become relatively objective. You have to have a tough exterior. It is a high-pressured environment and sometimes the support is there, but sometimes it isn't.

At work, I feel safe. I know that my colleagues are abiding by the same infection controls I am, but I struggle with the general attitude of the public. I hear my neighbours complaining about self-isolating, talking about their desperation to get out but then have people to stay over at their house and it makes me angry. It's that kind of attitude that means people are dying alone in hospital.

We are being faced with things that we've never seen before. All I want to do is provide the best service I can. It's the frustration that makes me cry. We should be taking the time to make sure we're not just stabbing in the dark and doing things willy nilly, but looking for evidence, looking for things that are similar. There were so many occasions where the pressure to see patient after patient after patient just meant that kind of care just wasn't possible. It was impossible to take a step back and think, "How best can I manage this patient?" They will have suffered because of that. I hated it.

You don't usually put your own health on the line when you go to work, but the immediate sense of physical danger, the exposure to infection is happening every single day.

David Oliver
Consultant physician in geriatric and acute general internal medicine.
May 2020

I've been a consultant in two different hospitals now for 22 years. I'm in my mid fifties, but I'm still very much on the shop floor and at the coalface, but I've never seen anything quite like this pandemic in my entire career. You're not usually putting your own health on the line when you come to work, but this immediate sense of physical danger and the exposure to infection are what we are facing every single day. It is an unprecedented situation. You don't know how you're going to handle that.

I was at a health summit in February 2020 with Matt Hancock and Chris Murphy, who was then the Chief Medical Officer, and a whole host of journalists. They were only allowed one question each about coronavirus. They were trying desperately to get some answers but back then, there was just a strange calmness. The key figures kept saying, "It's not here yet and we're in a 'contain, delay, mitigate' phase." In other words, "there is nothing to see here, now move on." But there was a strong sense that the situation wasn't being escalated enough or confronted, yet the World Health Organization had already declared it a global pandemic. Four days later, we had the first case.

Early March, we all started to realise how bad this was going to be. By mid-March, every patient was a Covid patient, one after the other.

It was relentless. It was like getting used to wartime conditions. You came onto the ward in scrubs, wearing protective equipment, washing your hands time and time and time again. This became our new reality. We all saw what was happening in Italy and New York City and Spain. They were being overwhelmed, and we didn't have quick access to testing at this point. It was taking days to get any results back. We didn't have PPE and we were trying desperately to get hold of it.

In a matter of weeks, we saw a complete reorganisation of how our health service and hospitals worked. Within three months, we'd tripled our intensive care unit capacity, and completely reconfigured the emergency system and changed the layouts of the wards. Everybody was wearing scrubs. Everybody was in protective equipment, and people had completely changed their jobs. But there was no more kneeling on the floor next to a patient's bed, no more comforting of families, or establishing a bond with people. We were speaking to them in protective masks and visors and goggles on computers. People felt abandoned.

I've never known a national response like it. When I was a teenager during the Falklands War, I remember the regular briefings about how many troops had been killed, but I can't remember any other time when there was a daily briefing about fatalities. This was indeed a national crisis, and still is. My wife is worried every single day. We haven't used the same kitchen or the same bedroom throughout the pandemic. She got in the car with me for the first time yesterday. That's not happened for eight weeks. Every day I worry that I am going to bring the virus home and infect her, yet I still do it. She knows what I'm like. She knows I will volunteer to work on any Covid ward and I won't be as careful as I should be about wearing the PPE, because if one of my patients says they can't hear me through it then I will pull it down so they can. We do it because we've got a very strong sense of loyalty to our patients. We have a very strong commitment. We feel very loyal to the NHS. It's like being in the military or the police.

I've seen some distressing things at the height of the pandemic that I don't want to see again. Large numbers of older people dying very quickly, one after the other, confused and bewildered and without their relatives present. I used to be a heavy drinker but gave it up. It's been a big deal for me not to be tempted again and use alcohol as a coping mechanism.

Despite everything bad this pandemic has done, there have been some positives. It has allowed the NHS to focus on people once again. The bureaucracy normally gets in the way. It's probably similar to what happened in wartime. Some things are never going to be the same again, and we are still worried about a second peak. One day I did get very upset though. Five of my patients died, one after the other, on a Saturday morning. That meant phone calls to families dressed from head to toe in PPE which makes it so hard to give them the compassion they need dressed like that. I came home and cried that day. We do cry.

Healthcare is a joint venture. It's not about egos, and I think it's brought a lot of the teams closer together. If I'm brutally honest, I would also say that it has revived me. If you're doing the same job day in, day out, week in, week out, it can be like Groundhog Day, but it's really refreshed my interest in clinical and scientific medicine, and I've been able to just focus on really sick people once again, which is what I'm trained for.

So much of this pandemic has made me angry though. The bloody Nightingale hospitals which have barely had any patients. The miracle of this pandemic has been that within a matter of weeks we've tripled in terms of care capacity, we've reconfigured the way our emergency departments run, we've reconfigured all of the beds, we've got people to change their job plans, change their actual jobs and change their hours, and often they were doing all of this without enough protective equipment. We've also not had enough testing, but they just cracked on and reorganised their work.

The NHS hasn't been overwhelmed, but that has had nothing to do with the Government. It's down to the actions of the leaders within the Health Service and the staff. We feel like we've been seriously let down by a shambolic Cabinet. The Government failed on PPE and failed to protect social care. Social care funding has been a problem for years, yet now people are suddenly interested. The Government has managed it all badly, the Government agencies have managed it badly. People appreciate honesty and straightforwardness and they haven't been giving that to the public.

What's got me through this, and where I've drawn hope, is the fact the NHS wasn't overwhelmed, and the camaraderie that exists within it. It has made us more secure. We have been given a bit of power back and I'm hoping that when we come out the other side, some of the gains we've made will stick. Frontline clinical staff and operation managers have been liberated and just cracked on with it. Hopefully it won't go back to business as usual. We are better than that.

Back in March, we were learning on the job, dealing with a new condition and a new way of working. It was adrenaline fuelled. If we get a second surge we will know what to do. It might even be fun for the first few weeks, everybody in scrubs again, everyone in protective gear, people doing different work. But if this goes on week after week, month after month, with a lot of people not doing their usual work, people will get exhausted. People close to the end of their career might just say they've had enough. If it drags on, I think it will be very difficult and it will put too much of a strain on staff.

I always wanted to be a doctor. I grew up with a dad who was an NHS doctor in Manchester and I've never regretted my choice, not ever. I am glad I was there.

I felt scared, anxious and apprehensive at first but then I thought, if not now then when? This is what I trained for.

Daniel Brooke
Sports & exercise medicine registrar.
Redeployed to A&E.
May 2020

I felt scared, anxious and apprehensive at first but then I thought, if not now then when? This is what I trained for. In these desperate situations, we can offer our skills and help out as much as possible. It kept going around my head, "if not now then when? What other event would make you drop things and go back to the frontline?"

But there was also a huge fear of the unknown, a nagging in the back of my mind. We knew so little about this virus and it was affecting some young people like me. I was going into a new department, with new staff, fighting a new virus. I'd never done this role before, I didn't know my surroundings, their systems, their protocols. I didn't know where things were, how things worked, and there was also the possibility I'd catch it, get ill and take it home to my family.

I'm 37. I ran the London Marathon last year, so I'm pretty fit, but there is still that thought in the back of your mind that ultimately, we don't know a lot about this virus, and it can affect young people, and when I read the projected statistics that 500,000 people could die from it, the realisation set in that this could be bad.

I got anxious about my parents, my three-year-old, the kind of "hot zones" I might be deployed to, but I did learn to rationalise it. I felt like I needed to be helping out. There were real concerns about staffing numbers so I put my anxieties aside. So often the anxiety ahead of an event is worse than the event itself. I just needed to get myself over that first barrier and get involved in the race.

There have been some amazingly brave people who have done so much more than me. I would say that I'm pretty resilient and robust, and I'm often able to thrive in difficult, challenging circumstances. In this case, the adrenalin got most of us through.

I've always wanted a career and a life that is fulfilling, and I want to feel like I am doing some good and having some kind of positive impact. You don't get into medicine for the financial return and you have to make a lot of sacrifices, but stepping up to the plate in a global pandemic is what I got into medicine for. We dealt with acutely unwell people and were able to do something profound to help them.

I got home one Friday night and my neighbours were having a fucking street party. There was absolutely no social distancing going on. It completely undermined everything I'd done that day.

Katie Ward
Consultant in respiratory and general medicine.
Seconded to the Nightingale Hospital.
May 2020

It was like waiting for a tsunami. We all knew it was coming. A week before it really hit, we had stopped all of our patients coming in and we started to get ready.

Right now, we are all very, very tired and we've seen lots of people die, and we're all asking questions. Should we have allowed more patients in hospitals? Did we make the right decisions? So may people died in nursing homes and didn't come to hospital, should we have admitted them or kept them in care homes away from the other patients? It's just so difficult to know. Did we do the right thing? How should we do it differently next time? Because there will be a next time.

Both my son and I had it but I never thought we were going to die. It felt like a really bad flu. I had a horrible cough, sinus pain, facial pain and lost my sense of taste, but after ten days I went back to work. I was fortunate, but we've had nurses die, pharmacists die. It has just been terrible.

This period has been like no other I've ever worked through because it has infringed on our personal lives too. There have been the added burdens of home-schooling, scrambling to get food, queuing up after 18 hour shifts to get into the supermarkets, and there's been no escaping it. It's on the radio all the time, my neighbours are asking me about it every day. There is no way of shutting it out at all. I work with it. I live with it. Even when I drive to work I'm aware of it. There's an eeriness to the streets, because there are so few people around.

It's the not knowing when it's going to finish that I struggle with. I can deal with change, but I find it really difficult dealing with uncertainty. I find myself worrying about the patients in the community who I normally care for that we just can't at the moment because we are too worried about bringing them into hospital. There isn't enough testing, so how can we protect them?

The big worry is that asymptomatic people are spreading it before they even come down with it. What does that mean for everyone? I'm too scared to think about it.

This is so different to how we usually work. In the winter, when we have to deal with huge demand, we know it will stop by Easter. If things are busy generally, or you're on call, you can take days off and recover, and get away from it all. But this is relentless. I can normally recuperate when my kids are at school and have a lie down, but they're at home all the time now. They're with me all the time, and they come with their own stress. They're very nice, and I love them, but they're seven and nine-yea- old boys who are like caged animals. There is no break at home and there is nowhere to go. If I'm not working on the ward then I'm standing in long queues at the supermarket, I'm tripping over piles of dirty clothes in the hallway, I'm resorting to KFC or pizza for my sons' dinners. It's just very difficult.

I'm not easily scared but this pandemic has frightened me. We have always worked with patients with flu, and we often work with tuberculosis and people with drug-resistant TB. It means that we've worked with PPE before, but we've never been properly fitted for it, and it doesn't fit people who are naturally skinny. It doesn't fit women very well. It doesn't fit tiny Filipino nurses very well. That brings with it, a big fear factor.

The Government's handling of this crisis has made me very angry. It has been shocking. The NHS has performed incredibly well but that hasn't got anything to do with the Government. We should have had adequate PPE, but they didn't stockpile it because they didn't want to spend the money. It should have been centrally held and centrally distributed, and all arranged through one centralized government. Instead, big hospitals were competing with a care home down the road that was competing with a GP surgery that was competing with a community hospital that was competing with a charity. Then, when we got it, it didn't even fit us properly. It was a total shit show.

I volunteered for the Nightingale Hospital because we thought we were going to get about 500 patients. We ended up treating just 50. It was an impressive achievement to get it up and running and feeling and working like a proper hospital so quickly, but who knows if it was the right decision. You just do the best you can at the time.

What I found most testing was public attitude though. I got home one Friday night, and my neighbours were having a fucking street party. It absolutely enraged me.

I had spent all day treating patients with tracheostomies, seeing patients who'd been on ventilators for weeks who were just about coming round, and then I went home and there was absolutely no social distancing going on. It completely undermined everything that I'd done that day.

Nothing I do on the ward will stop the spread. That's down to the public. We have no real treatment at this point. There is no vaccine. We have no way out of this. Nothing has changed apart from people have stayed at home so the virus hasn't transferred to others as easily.

I have elderly parents. There's no reason to suggest that my mum won't get it next week and she'll probably die if she gets it. It is quite a struggle to get your head around this crap, and it's those same people who are not social distancing that are clapping me on a Thursday, then having their neighbours over on a Friday night. We're just so tired. We feel undermined by the Government and those who refuse to respect social distancing.

But there aren't many jobs that you can do that are at a high academic level and challenge your brain every day that also get an immediate, human response. I can always do something to make someone feel better, and that is rewarding.

We didn't know who was going to survive Covid and who wasn't. We knew there was a chance we could catch it, so if that day came, we wanted to be husband and wife. That was all that mattered.

Jann Tipping
Acute care nurse.
April 2020

Our big day should have had 200 people from around the world celebrating with us. Instead it was just the two of us, in the hospital chapel with our families watching on Zoom.

Annalan and I met four years ago when I was a student nurse and he was a consultant at King's College Hospital in London, and I was training at Guy's and St Thomas'. Now, we both work in acute medicine and are on the same team. We have to be level headed working together. We have to be professionals, but our colleagues find it hilarious.

It was at the end of February as the virus started to progress rapidly that we started to understand the risk our wedding could pose to our friends and family. My younger sister is vulnerable and high risk.

As the scale of the spread increased and it started to move from country to country, we couldn't bear the thought of putting those closest to us at risk, so we cancelled it. It was actually a real relief. It meant nobody was going to put themselves in danger for us. All of a sudden we could just get married whenever we wanted because it was only us who would be there. There was no sadness or regret. We just wanted it to happen sooner rather than later. Doing the job we do we are aware that there are no guarantees. We didn't know who was going to survive Covid and who wasn't. There was no certainty where Covid was concerned. We knew there was a chance we could catch it, so if that day came, we wanted to be husband and wife. That was all that mattered.

We go to the hospital every day. I'd met the chaplain there before and she just made everything possible. We felt like it was the right place to be. We got married at the height of lockdown when nobody was leaving their house to do anything but go to work or buy food. It felt like at any moment someone could just say, "this can't happen," because the rules and regulations around the pandemic were constantly changing.

As the day got nearer, we worried that one of the witnesses would get a fever or the chaplain would get sick, or we would get the virus. It wasn't until the moment we were standing in front of each other in the hospital chapel that it felt real. It felt too good to be true. It was such a magical day. We had so much fun, and were surprised by how much it felt like a wedding, even without people being there.

We got ready together in the morning at home. I did my own hair, but Annalan helped me put the bow in it. I'd ordered three dresses, one of them didn't arrive in time, the other had a huge stain on it when it arrived and the other was the wrong size. Four days before the wedding, I still didn't have a dress to wear. I didn't know what I was going to do.

One of my friends, who is a wedding photographer, spoke to a couple of her contacts and I sent my measurements to a shop, gave them an idea of what I wouldn't wear and they found something in my size and posted it to me. It arrived. It was gorgeous, but it was far too long for me. I'm short, so I had to carry the huge train in a big ball. I was trying my best to look graceful but then also carrying metres of fabric over my shoulder. It wasn't quite how I envisaged my wedding day but now it feels special. It adds to our story and is all part of the memories.

We travelled to the church separately because we weren't allowed to get the same Uber taxi. Annalan went ahead of me, but I ended up being really, really late and stuck in traffic. He didn't know where I was for ages. I also wasn't allowed to wear my dress outside of the chapel. So I arrived at the hospital in normal clothes and then had to get changed. At one point, I was in my dress and standing outside the chaplain's office on my own in my outfit with people I work with walking past me. They looked totally baffled and kept asking me what on earth I was doing there.

Our families watched the service on Zoom which was strange. We knew they were watching but you couldn't see their smiles or their expressions so you didn't know what they were thinking or what they were doing. Afterwards, we had a Zoom reception. We had dinner and champagne delivered to our flat. Everyone did their speeches and we had a first dance in our living room and everyone cheered. It was really lovely, really different but we are so happy with the day we had.

We are so pleased that all our family and friends are healthy. Everyone is still with us and we've been incredibly lucky. We don't feel like we were short-changed at all. We feel married and we definitely feel like we had a really wonderful wedding day that was right for us. I wouldn't change it for anything.

When we went back to work, an elderly patient on the ward knew about our wedding. She got really emotional whenever she saw us both together. We joked with her about having our honeymoon on the ward and she let out a real howl of laughter. It was wonderful, because when people come in with Covid, they are so nervous and tense. Their eyes are like saucers, but this lady felt relaxed enough to laugh. It was nice to hear that sound of joy in the hospital again.

Surgical masks and thin plastic aprons are simply not adequate PPE. I had colleagues tell me that they were fearing for their lives.

Adrienn Gyori
Junior doctor.
June 2020

At the beginning of April when I was due to start my third FY1 placement (which is the first year of foundation training after completing an undergraduate medicine degree) I was redeployed to intensive therapy unit (ITU), likely thanks to my previous experience on ITU and anaesthetics placements as a final-year medical student. While I was excited for the opportunity to work on ITU, I knew that the experience would have a huge impact on me, the consequences of which I would not fully appreciate until much later.

That first month on ITU was the most emotionally, mentally and physically challenged I had ever felt, only having had one comparable experience previously when I had undergone life-changing surgery. The coping mechanism was similar in that I largely repressed my acute emotional response, and focused purely on the mental and physical task at hand.

Initially I would work 13-hour shifts taking a single brief break halfway through. I would concentrate on being meticulous in my assessment of patients, in my use of PPE, in my approach to inserting arterial lines and later a central venous catheter, a tube that is inserted into the heart.

I had always felt at home in the slightly obsessive compulsive environment of critical care. I took every opportunity to learn, and I drove myself into exhaustion for fear of not being competent enough as the most junior doctor on ITU. I learned from my seniors as much as I could, and in turn tried to teach colleagues, mostly redeployed nursing staff, any skills or knowledge I had that they might find useful.

I tried to support friends and colleagues, tried to channel an inner voice of reason, despite sometimes just wanting to scream with anger, frustration and devastation. I have never been a person to procrastinate, but this reflection has taken me weeks to write, because thus far I have not been able to string together a half-coherent set of thoughts.

I am still feeling overwhelmed by the events of the past few months, and I often struggle to pinpoint the precise trigger for certain emotions that I experienced.

To make progress easier, I tried to identify individual experiences, and reflect on how they had made me feel and react.

The small, tight knit community of a hospital will never fail to be shaken by the death of one of its own. Sister M died of Covid only a few days after giving birth to a baby girl. I do not have the words to describe the grief, and I cannot even begin to understand how her family must feel. With time I hope they will find the strength to heal.

A Channel 4 report regarding Sister M's death: "The hospital said they had not experienced any significant shortages [in PPE]". In light of the obvious lack of adequate personal protective equipment (PPE) on many wards, about which concerns were repeatedly raised, and the death of a member of staff, this response from hospital management is inexcusable. If such a statement was indeed made, then it is a pitiful attempt to save face, rather than admit to a mistake, apologise, and act to prevent such a tragedy from happening again. Surely that is what would be in line with GMC good medical practice.

Soon after Sister M's death, Sister K also fell ill with Covid. She was admitted, struggling to maintain her oxygen levels. I went to visit this brave woman who had shown me so much kindness as I went through the growing pains of my first medical placement. Working hard to breathe through a nebuliser, Sister K waved at me enthusiastically, but I could see how scared she was. She knew what was coming if she got any worse, and we all knew the grim statistics associated with patients who required escalation to the high dependency unit (HDU) or ITU.

The next day she was admitted to HDU, and we braced ourselves for another tragedy. There was nothing to do but wait. During those days I often thought about the measures medical schools take to prepare doctors for dealing with deaths of patients. At UCL we were required to complete a cancer pathway project, which involved interviewing and following up an individually allocated patient receiving cancer treatment. The expectation was very much that many students would experience the death of their patient, not just any patient they had come across in passing, but a patient they had built rapport with over a longer period of time. It felt cruel, but necessary. However, we were not similarly equipped to deal with deaths of colleagues.

I think this is why being on the frontline of the Covid pandemic required so much resilience, what we experienced went so far beyond our normal coping mechanisms. It was impossible to leave work at work, because what made work hard impacted every other aspect of our lives, and the disease that threatened our patients posed an equal risk to our families, friends and colleagues. Sister K was stepped down from HDU, and eventually discharged from hospital. I was not there the day she went home, but I saw the recording, the hospital corridors lined with staff applauding and crying as she was being wheeled to the front door. I cried with relief as well. Sister K going home was a spark of joy in very dark times.

This is another devastating case that I came across on ITU. We had a father and son admitted with Covid around the same time. They had been isolating at home together, but both started experiencing severe respiratory symptoms and both had viral pneumonitis confirmed on imaging, "classic Covid" as it became known on clerking documents.

The father was in his early seventies, with hypertension and diabetes, comorbidities associated with worse prognosis, which was a trend we were noticing early on. The son was in his early forties, admitted with no past medical history.

Looking at him, and many other younger patients on ITU there was a very prevalent common finding: obesity.

In general terms, patients on ITU could be split into three groups: 1) Young but obese patients, some with diabetes, but often without other comorbidities, 2) Patients with underlying lung disease such as asthma, chronic obstructive pulmonary disease, or long-term smoking, 3) Older patients with associated comorbidities such as hypertension, diabetes, heart disease or kidney disease.

Generally, we understood the risk factors that made it more likely for a patient to require ITU escalation. However, once on ITU we had a much poorer understanding of which patients would recover and which would not. Our statistics for the large part remained grim, at best one in three patients were stepped down successfully from ITU, but at the height of the Covid pandemic it could be as few as one in five.

Intubated Covid patients often did not follow a predictable trajectory. We could see drastic deterioration within a matter of minutes, a patient's oxygen requirement would suddenly increase, and despite persistent maximal oxygen therapy their blood gases would show no sign of recovery. We already knew that they had severe acute respiratory distress syndrome (ARDS), but the trigger for such rapid change was poorly understood. Sadly, we observed this lack of predictability with the father and son who were admitted. The father was doing poorly from the beginning, and in truth we did not expect him to survive. The son, however, had been improving significantly, his oxygen requirements had decreased and there was talk of transitioning him onto a tracheostomy to allow for gradual weaning off sedation. But early one morning he dropped off the edge of a cliff, perhaps a young body running out of energy to compensate. Ventilatory support was eventually withdrawn and he died. His father outlived him by a few days.

I looked after this patient for the better part of six weeks, monitoring his painstakingly slow progress. He had been intubated for severe ARDS, his kidneys had stopped working, and he was regularly running dangerously high temperatures. His partner called diligently every afternoon, a gentle, kind voice that despite his own agony never failed to ask me how I was doing.

When he called, I would at times hold the phone to my patient's ear so that his partner could talk to him. I would not have the heart to move for a good while. The last time I spoke to him, he told me that they had been together for over thirty years, and were going to get married in the summer. A few days later I came onto shift and found the bed empty, the patient's name not on the board. I felt a lump in my throat, fearing the worst. Thankfully, he had been stepped down and transferred to another hospital for dialysis. I was so relieved, but sad that I could not wish him well before he left.

For days all I could think about was their wedding, I really hope they will make it happen, and though I will never know for sure, I want to think that their story has a happy end.

This is an aspect of the Covid experience that I am persistently angry about. The response of the trust, of Public Health England (PHE) and of the Government to the lack of appropriate PPE has been largely infuriating.

The country's stash of PPE was mostly privately owned, acquiring some from overseas ended in failure, the Government opted out of the European PPE scheme, and PHE "adjusted" its advice to reflect the national shortage rather than adhere to World Health Organisation guidance. Surgical masks, or FFP1, and thin plastic aprons are simply not adequate PPE, regardless of what PHE and the government wish to believe. On the frontline there is enough evidence to suggest that a significant proportion of the staff using this menial level of protection contracted Covid and many became very ill. I had colleagues tell me that they were fearing for their lives. Others worried about being asymptomatic carriers who might infect their parents and families.

On ITU PPE was largely adequate, although occasionally FFP3 masks did run out, and there was a period while we were told that single use surgical gowns would be washed and recycled. We also noticed that masks with an expiry date in 2014 had been rebranded, a new sticker obscuring the original expiry date. Why? Just tell us honestly that this is all the trust has available. Why assume we are not going to notice? This incident just added to the already escalating sense of distrust and apprehension.

"Clap for our NHS heroes" is probably one of the most nausea-inducing statements from the Government during the Covid pandemic.

Firstly, there is nothing heroic about turning up to work, and doing so with a certain level of integrity, I wish more politicians took note of this. Secondly, please do not clap. Those in power clapping is not going to protect us from the phenomenal failure in providing frontline workers with adequate protection. I appreciate the clapping from the well-meaning public, and it would be a lie to say that I was left cold by the Thursday evening display from the police and the fire services, frontline staff who are much in the same boat as the NHS. However, the leaders of this country using a seemingly innocent gesture as a political gimmick is infuriating.

We have no use for that sort of farce and façade. I find myself circling back to PPE again. Each individual glove being counted as an individual item of PPE is just embarrassing. The health secretary implying that shortage is due to PPE being wasted reflects a deep-seated lack of insight. More recently, the exposure of a senior Government official driving to visit relatives during lockdown, and giving the pitiful excuse of wishing to test his eyesight, just confirms that different sets of rules apply to those with power and those without.

This particular incident added insult to injury for many people who struggled with physical and mental health, death and illness of loved ones, financial insecurity, and the depressingly long stretch of social isolation over the past months.

I have written about my most well-defined memories from the past two months, but there are plenty more that will inevitably bubble to the surface, take shape and need addressing. Certainly this level of compartmentalisation has helped me to understand and digest my Covid experience. I have tried to be introspective as events were unfolding, but it was easier to remain objective and not address the immense emotional burden of the situation until later. Afterwards, I would spend hours talking with close friends, family and my partner.

Initially I would just cry in the safety of my home, struggling to find the words for what I was experiencing. But eventually, with plenty of coaxing, thoughts began to take shape, and finally after a very long conversation with an old friend and fellow doctor, I broke through my mental barrier and started writing.

It is very much a release I needed, in many ways the first step to gaining closure.

In the future, we will look back on this period with great sadness, and questions will be asked, but the NHS response is something we can all be proud of.

Ed Jabbari
Clinical research training fellow in the Department of Clinical and Movement Neurosciences. Volunteered to Covid ward.
May 2020

Like most of my medical colleagues, the beginning of March was spent trying to convince friends and family that life was going to be very different, very soon. All the while we continued in our regular roles, which for me was in a non-clinical capacity finalising research projects as part of the PhD that I had been working towards for the past four years.

As the daily new cases started to increase and lockdown was imposed, I struggled to grasp the scale at which the shape of the frontline was changing to adapt to the demands on the NHS. Suddenly my research didn't seem that important and instead I was reconnecting with friends who were working in key areas like A&E and the intensive care unit to listen to their experiences. Our regular calls were a source of support but also a period of reflection and realisation that we were in the eye of a storm.

Then, like all other research doctors, I was asked if I would volunteer to be redeployed to work on the wards. The response to this call to arms was overwhelming and a reflection of just how much everyone wanted to do their bit. My nervousness had already amplified in the lead up to my first shift as both my partner (a neurological physiotherapist) and aunt (an intensive care nurse) had been hit by symptoms, presumably, given the nature of their work, caused by Covid-19. They later received positive test results.

When I eventually made it to the ward, it was unlike anything I had experienced: the wearing of PPE for every single patient, the difficult phone conversations with family members who weren't allowed to visit the hospital to see their relatives and, of course, the genuine fear that you could be the next healthcare worker to get unwell.

What I'd also never seen to this extent, however, and what ultimately got me through this period, was the spirit and camaraderie of everyone on the frontline, from the doctors to the security men and women guarding the front door. In the face of such uncertainty, everyone piled in, supported each other and did their best because that's what we're hardwired to do – pandemic or not. There is no doubt that in the future we will look back on this period with great sadness and questions will rightly continue to be asked about the government's handling of the situation. But let it be known that the NHS response is something we can all be proud of.

Covid highlighted the need to look after staff so they can look after patients. That need was there before Covid and that need will be enduring.

Neil Greenberg, Derek Tracy & Mark Tarn
Occupational psychologists.
Led the Mental Health staff support strategy at London Nightingale Hospital.
June 2020

State of the art computers without logins, enough free Mango Coke to bathe in, and daily exposure to the vulnerabilities of the Human Condition. These were just some of our experiences that surrounded our time at the London Nightingale Hospital.

We were called up to help establish a mental health strategy for the hospital, alongside setting-up a mental health team to respond to staff wellbeing in what was anticipated to be a hugely testing environment. The figures were stark: potentially 4,000 patients – all critically unwell – and 16,000 staff providing care for them. We could see the emerging situation in other countries such as Italy, and the progression of Covid-19 heading towards us seemed clear and inevitable. We were tasked to support staff, thus helping to improve the quality of the care they would provide. This was a clear opportunity for mental health providers to make a substantial impact, and by doing so ensure the frontline staff performed to the best of their abilities.

Then there was the shock and awe at the scale of the Nightingale operation. It was impossible not to be overwhelmed walking into the ExCel in those early days, the exhibition centre was rapidly evolving into a hospital, the biggest hospital in post-war Britain. A kilometre long, 41 wards on each side of the building, each 42 beds deep.

As the military and other contractors set about the herculean task of getting this ready for the first patients in just over a week, the nature of support that the frontline staff might need sharpened considerably. But there were advantages in what we were trying to do, not least because we were on the ground floor, able to establish the mental health team as an integral core part from the beginning. On top of this, perhaps uniquely in our time in healthcare, we had a blank slate, relatively limitless resources, and an inherent trust that our views and experience would be respected.

Two terms were key in our work: "moral injury" and "post-traumatic growth".

Moral injury derives from military settings, and describes the phenomenon where individuals face scenarios that ethically challenge their core sense of competency and fairness. Most of the time in healthcare individuals of different professional groups and experience levels slot into well-established roles in well-established teams. The job in hand and the expectations upon one are clear, even if arduous. But with Covid-19, things were different, rapidly changing guidelines, concerns about the availability of PPE, very unwell patients with high mortality rates, inexperienced staff working in technical settings, concerns about picking up the illness and perhaps infecting one's family.

All of this at a time when fewer social supports were available for us all, with social distancing and the shut-down of bars, restaurants, and all those other places to which we turn. The risks to staff were clear, and moral injury can lead to various forms of mental illness, from depression and anxiety to post-traumatic stress disorder.

The other term is important too – post-traumatic growth. The evidence from other traumas, terrorist attacks and so-forth, is that mental illness is the exception, and that most individuals would grow and develop through their experiences of providing care during the pandemic, however unwished for that it might be.

The science was there, the challenge for us at the time, for all services, was how to nudge the needle as much towards growth and away from injury. The model was a stepped-care approach. Starting at induction with honest, frank, non-sugar coated information on the challenges faced. This was not a time to shy away from the difficulties ahead, but a moment for staff to consider what they were up against, and the individual pressures and supports they had in their own lives.

Accurate up-to-date information was supplied on resources. It's an unfortunate truth that in healthcare, information is often neither accurate nor up-to-date. Staff were inducted on how it was "ok to not be ok", and talked through the concepts of injury and growth, as well as being congratulated on what they had stepped up for. The next task was encouraging staff on shifts to be buddied-up, with a named person to look out for, and who would look out for you. This was to be another way of ensuring an eye was kept on staff, the other important eye being that of the normal managerial chain of command.

Walking the floor, dropping in to post-shift hand-overs, we were fortunate to have some furloughed staff from the airline industry, folk whose expertise and skills in engaging people in a friendly chat perhaps surpassed that of even mental health professionals, though they had to revise their normal more tactile approach.

"Nip it in the bud" was the message, as was the encouragement for managers to engage in psychologically-savvy conversations with their team. We were very clear that the science was strongly supportive of the psychologically protective nature of mutually supportive teams. In essence, rather than focussing on trying to create psychologically tough individuals, we did all we can to create psychologically robust health teams.

Of course, some staff needed more than that, and our mental health team comprised both mental health nurses and psychiatrists capable of carrying out formal reviews. What was perhaps most pleasing about this was the immediacy of the service. No booking in or referral forms were needed. Dropping in was fine.

We were on site and ready. The principle was a de-medicalised approach of getting people back to the front line where suitable, which was the vast majority of the time. The Nightingale had a persona of a flexible and focused unit that would combat those who suffered with the virus. It was unlike any other hospital any of us have worked in peacetime, if you've seen the ExCel Centre you might have a sense of why.

Perhaps the final complexity was the stand-down. It became clear that, at least in this first wave, the hospital would not be required. Good news, right? Well of course. Yet for staff on the ground it carried more emotional resonance than just gratitude.

They stood up and volunteered to do something amazing, in the end that was not required in the way they had imagined. Friendships had been formed, learning had occurred, now we were being told we were not needed. The final day of reflection for us at the O2 arena was a chance to hold a remembrance of those patients we had looked after, including those who had died, the impact on their friends and families and the impact on us.

The Nightingale was enlightened in incorporating staff well-being into its core philosophy. Not all units or hospitals are like this. It is a question for services going forward: Covid is an example – a severe one – of a profound shock to a system, but others will undoubtedly occur.

Covid highlighted the need to look after staff so that they can look after patients. That need was there before Covid and that need will be enduring. Our experience was that it is completely possible to build mental health support into the DNA of a healthcare unit. What's more, morally it's the right thing to do. Perhaps then the Nightingale mental health staff support experience will not be wasted, instead it may provide a blueprint for how other healthcare facilities can properly provide support to their staff in the years ahead.

When that first patient collapsed, there were no warning signs. It all happened within minutes. I knew then that we were going to struggle.

Waleed Fawzi
Consultant geriatric psychiatrist.
May 2020

I first took notice of Covid in early March when I spoke to my sister (a doctor in Chicago). She warned me about how serious this virus was going to be. She had a colleague from Wuhan who gave a very bleak account and told her things were much worse than what we knew at the time. She knew I worked with old people and asked how we were preparing for this. I didn't have any plans at the time as I didn't think it was going to be serious and didn't imagine it was going to have the impact it did. By mid March I was thinking that I would have to stop visitors from coming to my ward. I was slowly coming to the realisation that If my elderly patients caught it, it would be disastrous. I escalated my concern and they were immediately informed and we stopped visits. I also realised I had to look after myself. It was a question of when I was going to get sick and not if. I started exercising regularly and went for long runs. I also tried to reduce my exposure, by reducing non-essential contact with patients and colleagues. This was my approach to managing personal risk.

That same week a patient was transferred from another hospital. Covid testing for asymptomatic patients was not in place and the lady was well when she was admitted. She suddenly collapsed and had to be resuscitated whilst we were waiting for an ambulance to arrive. The usual five minute wait stretched to 50. She was admitted to hospital and three days later we found out it was Covid, miraculously she survived. Covid is not like anything my team and I have experienced before. The strong sense of realisation came when that first patient collapsed, as there were no warning signs. It all happened within minutes. I knew then that we were going to struggle. By the end of the following week we had a Covid ward for elderly patients suffering from serious mental illness. Our colleagues at the general hospital stepped in to support us in looking after patients. We lost three patients out of 20 which is a reasonable outcome considering their age and frailty. These were incredibly difficult times.

By the end of March, I developed low grade fever and felt severe exhaustion. I was one of the first NHS staff to get tested in early April and the result was positive. We were not using face masks routinely at the time and the guidance on PPE use was still being developed. My whole family was eventually sick including our 1 year old who spiked a 40 degree temperature. We were very lucky. One of my colleagues was in intensive care for over two months. He has not been well enough to return to work since. It was horrendous and heartbreaking for the team to see our colleague suffering. I am in awe of all my colleagues who came to work on Covid wards day in day out knowing the chances of catching it are high, and the consequences are very serious. Some of my colleagues were terrified of coming to work and a few retired, but most just got on with it and continued to provide the same care as if nothing had changed.

It was Covid's rapid spread, patient deterioration and symptom severity that I found so shocking. There was a sense of foreboding going to work, but I felt the need to be there and be seen every day in the hospital, to look after my patients and support my colleagues. The number of people who died was shocking, sadly this was a perfect storm which we did not expect or prepare for.

You were washing your hands every five minutes, and you would reach a point where your skin was falling off.

William Rickitts
Consultant chest physician.
May 2020

Our respiratory wards normally deal with one or two high-dependency patients at a time, but at the peak we were dealing with 20 to 30, dressed in full PPE for 12 hour shifts, in the suits, the full length gowns, the masks, getting hot and sweaty all day every day, and there were so many tiers of complexity and everything was changing so rapidly. It was exhausting. It has been insanely busy, absolutely draining, but it's been incredibly rewarding seeing the whole hospital pull together with a single, common goal. Doctors, nurses, consultants have all been thrown into new ways of working with no notice and just cracked on with it. In a weird way, it's been an amazing time to work. The medicine has been horrible though. Tough. Such sick patients. Really, really sick. When I look around the ward normally and see twenty patients, I know half a dozen of them will be well and waiting to go home, most of them will be moderately unwell but heading in the right direction and a couple will be really sick but during Covid, all of them were really sick patients.

We had a phase when we just had no good news stories. Everyone was either getting sick or going to intensive care. It felt like we were never discharging anybody. Psychologically that was very difficult for a lot of people. It was very intense, and there was no relief. You didn't leave the ward for a whole day, even your food was brought to you, so switching off was impossible. Normally, if I have a bad day at work, I get on the train, I read my book, I debrief with my wife, I put it to bed. I'll go to football, I'll shout at the opposition, at the referee, but all of a sudden those normal coping mechanisms weren't there. Also with Covid, you go home, everyone on the tube is wearing a face mask, you put the television on, the news is all about Covid, you go on social media, everything is about Covid. My wife is a physiotherapist and her day is all about Covid too. A bad day used to be, you had a disagreement with a colleague, a patient you'd become fond of deteriorated or died, or you didn't perform well in a meeting. But a Covid bad day was you'd have 24 patients, all of whom were really, really sick with none of them getting better. Everything was a lot more intense, and so many patients were dying.

My default position is not to get overly emotional about things, but when we got our first confirmed case, I was on the ward round, and I remember it so clearly. There was a guy who had pneumonia who just kept getting worse, which was unexpected. At the time, you only got tested for Covid if you ended up in intensive care, which he did. He only got a test because it was policy. Nobody actually thought he had it. I got a phone call at home late on the Saturday night to tell me he'd tested positive. I then had to tell 40 members of staff who'd been in contact with him to isolate. All we could do was keep our fingers crossed.

When I went back to work after ten days, the wards were filling up fast. There were so many Covid patients coming in. You were washing your hands every five minutes, and you would reach a point where your skin was falling off. I started off washing my hands in water at normal temperature and was teasing my registrar because he'd use the sink after me and kept turning the temperature down. He'd say to me, "You think I'm a wimp don't you? But just you wait. I'll give you two or three days of washing your hands like this, every minute of every day." He was right, your hands fall apart and you can't cope with warm water because it burns. Your hands are completely raw from the washing. If you're looking after 24 patients and see each of them twice a day, and you're washing your hands before and after each patient, that's nearly 100 hand washes a day. It hurts.

I don't know how you define success in times like these. I spent six months working in a military hospital a long time ago and the most significant difference I noticed then was their "can do" attitude. Sometimes the NHS can be a bit sluggish, but when it came to Covid, the overriding sense was, "It will work, and we're going to make it work, come hell or high water." As doctors, we are used to fixing things, we like to feel that we have proactively made a difference, but to see hundreds of patients at a time when there is no fix, or a proven treatment, was psychologically very difficult. It goes against everything you're used to feeling as a doctor. It was not what you normally think of as medicine.

I've been in this job nearly 20 years, and you can often look at a patient at the end of the bed and get a vibe about whether they will pull through or not. Patients will start on a trajectory and follow that trajectory. They will either get worse despite what you do, and you prepare for the worst, or they will respond to treatment and get better. Very occasionally things go wrong, but rarely. It just wasn't like that with Covid patients. I don't know the physiology of why this was, but lots of medics said it. You'd think your patients were getting better, and suddenly they'd get worse, and this could quite often happen more than once. It shattered what I thought I knew. I always thought I could tell who was getting better, who was getting worse, who had a good prognosis, who had a bad prognosis, and all of a sudden, I couldn't predict with the same degree of accuracy.

I think my worst day was one Monday when there was a sense that things were starting to wind down. It was a very odd week. We still had a ward full of very sick people. They were the sickest of the sick. Within an hour of starting, I'd sent two patients to intensive care and I couldn't hear myself think because people started to come at me from all angles. I was going from one bed to the next, trying to see to them in a logical order but every five minutes a nurse or a physio or the ICU team would come and get me to go and see someone else who was even sicker. You'd go and see them, then you'd try to get back to your round, and someone else would come over because someone else had deteriorated. It went on like that until the end of my shift. That was my hardest day. It was cognitive overload. I didn't have time to think. I was just being bombarded with information about how sick these people were, and how the hell do you decide which sick patient is of higher priority. It's like military crisis resource management. You're trying to juggle resources and staff. Your brain is so wired when you finish a shift like that that you can't switch off and go to sleep properly. Your brain just continues to buzz. It is constantly thinking.

Only in time, will I be able to process all what's happened, work out how to describe it and what to say. I heard a veteran say once, "I wasn't frontline. I didn't fly the planes, I only repaired them," even though he was repairing them in a war zone when bombs could have been dropped on him at any minute. I am not frontline. They guys in ICU are frontline. There's always someone more frontline than you.

124

Tears fall when our death notifications arrive, prompting memories of recent consultations with patients who've now died.

Mhairi McKittrick
GP.
April 2020

Tears come more easily these days.

Since the start of the pandemic we have all seen unprecedented changes in our lives. I was identified as needing to be shielded, due to a respiratory condition, and returned home from work one Tuesday in March to be told I was going to start working remotely from the following day and not to return to the practice for at least 12 to 14 weeks. One other GP colleague was in the same cohort but on holiday when I had to text her to break the news.

This in itself was a huge change, before you even consider the logistics of setting up a total triage system for all patients in the practice, splitting the staff in to clinical and non-clinical building locations, arranging hot and cold spaces within the practice for safe delivery of patient-facing care where absolutely necessary, starting daily Zoom team meetings, shifting to remote debriefs for my GP registrar and embracing video consulting's via AccuRx. I am now able, at the click of a button, to see parts of my patient's anatomy I never dreamt would be visible to me in my own home via my mobile phone!

The tears have come for various reasons, some expected, others less so. Assessing patients with worsening Covid symptoms by phone then video link has been harrowing: seeing their distress and yet unable to intervene apart from to identify that they are in the red category and arrange 999 transfer to hospital, meanwhile telling their family they cannot accompany them. The anguish on relatives' faces as they realise they may never see their loved one again is an image I can't forget.

One middle aged man with no risk factors caused me particular distress and left me questioning why this dreadful virus was wreaking havoc and destruction across the globe. I called his wife three days after his admission to check on his progress. She answered the phone and before I could even enquire about her husband she told me she was just sitting down to write me a letter of thanks. Despite her own worries about her sick husband on a CPAP airway machine in ITU she had taken the time to think of writing to me.

She went on to tell me in detail all the events that had unfolded following my video call, the kindness and sincerity of the paramedics, the fantastic telephone support line at the hospital who kept in in touch with all the updates on her husband, and the amazing ITU team who were caring for him. On the morning I called he had improved and they were starting to wean him off the CPAP machine.

Our practice WhatsApp has prompted tears of joy for the amazing team I am part of and the support and unending compassion they are showing in these challenging times, both to our patients and each other. The most heartfelt tears came when unexpectedly, on a Sunday afternoon, my phone rang. The headmaster at my daughter's school spoke to tell me that following my email asking if they could help make visors for our Primary Care Network he and the design technology lead had spent the weekend making 73 visors on the school laser printer and he wanted to know where to deliver them.

I was speechless, unable to express my immense gratitude for their generosity in giving their time and expertise to help support us in ensuring all our staff could remain safe whilst seeing patients. He was shocked by my tears, assuring me it was the least they could do. More tears fall when our death notifications arrive, prompting memories of recent consultations with patients who've now died.

Yet more, on reading the email confirming an outbreak of Covid in my father-in-law's care home. He is still well but fearful of, as he describes it, "catching the plague". I want to shed more tears of joy but know they may be interspersed with more tears of sadness over the coming weeks and months.

Covid-19 reminds me of HIV in the 1990s but on a scale that is 100 times greater, and within a period of six weeks, not six years.

Alan Salama
Professor of nephrology.
June 2020

The most incredible thing about Covid-19 was how we were learning about what it was one day at a time. It was like trying to learn how to fly a plane in midair. People die in hospital all the time, but the death rate from Covid was quite something. I've never had an experience on this scale. It reminded me of HIV when it started in the UK and we were scared. I was a registrar in the early 90s, looking after people coming into a general hospital. Some would come in with unusual symptoms. HIV had been around for maybe seven or eight years, but we hadn't really appreciated the variety of ways it could present itself and what it could mean. That was how our specialist HIV unit began to take shape, but we didn't have much in the way of treatment for it at that point. Covid-19 is very similar, but on a much greater scale, and it all happened within a period of six weeks, not six years.

Usually, in medicine, we know what we know, and we recognise patterns in the way people deal with certain diseases. Some things are less common and you have to think them through, but for the majority of diseases we see, there are patterns. Covid-19 was completely new. The patterns that we were told we should be looking out for weren't always there.

In the first few days most patients who came through the door had a cough and a fever and shortness of breath. But then we saw people who had tummy pains presented as though they had appendicitis or even a gall bladder or kidney infection, people who had no fever but who had chronic obstructive pulmonary disease (COPD). There were patients sitting in open wards with Covid-19, we just didn't realise that's what they had. At that stage we weren't even in our protective gear. The decision was made that we would only test patients who we thought were going to be bad enough to be admitted to the hospital. So, a big group were going back out into the community and they had Covid-19, but we hadn't confirmed it. We also weren't allowed to test staff, which was a really stupid mistake. We probably had staff spreading it too.

Public Health England said only ten percent of swabs could be for staff. Peeing in the ocean wouldn't describe it well enough. I have a lot of frustration about how we had to deal with it all blindfolded. There was the anxiety of not understanding what this was, how it was going to affect people and how many people were going to get affected. Was I going to end up catching it? Was I going to end up in intensive care? Was I going to end up dying? I think everyone working at the hospital felt this, although we didn't talk about it.

The kidney patients - my patients - were, unfortunately, disproportionately affected. We do a lot of transplants and many patients are immunosuppressed which means they take drugs that reduce their immune system to stop them rejecting their kidney. I deal with a lot of patients who have immunological diseases or auto-immune diseases that affect their kidneys, so we had a large proportion of people who had a greater risk of getting the virus badly. We also had the dialysis population coming in three times a week. I distinctly remember a meeting (the kidney consultants meet once a week), two weeks before the whole thing blew up and we closed the hospital to visitors and became a little fortress, where we said, "What are we going to do when a dialysis patient gets it? How are we going to stop this spreading?" On any one shift, you might have 30 people on dialysis, and that happens three times a day, six days a week. A colleague and I went through a list of patients, around 300 or 400 were on some kind of immunosuppression, and we had to decide whether they should be shielding, or whether they would be safe just to socially distance. At the end of March we were still doing kidney transplants but were acutely aware that we wanted to get these people who were very high risk out of the hospital as soon as possible. We had a number of very vulnerable patients who were on the ward, and who were, it turned out, sitting next to other patients who turned out to have Covid-19. We had to stop the transplant program because there was no way we could guarantee that we had clean, Covid-free areas in the hospital.

Two weeks later one of the last transplant patients, who was in his 40s, got re-admitted with very bad Covid-19 and ended up being ventilated. He was going to die. Transplantation is normally something that is such a positive process for us and for the patients. We see their quality of life being transformed. Patients are free again. So when it goes wrong, or when the process of transplantation ends up curtailing a life, it feels truly awful. It's not really guilt, but it makes us feel doubly bad that we have positively caused harm. But, we made a decision to try something a little bit experimental with this patient, and we don't know if it was that or luck, but he turned around, and left the hospital four weeks later. That was a standout moment for me. That was pretty cool.

At home I decided to isolate myself in the spare room for the first couple of weeks when I was covering the ward. I ate separately from my family. We were talking across the hallway. I kept myself to myself, which in retrospect seems a bit over the top but at the time I was acutely aware that I didn't want to come back with something and then give it to the whole family. I would leave a set of clothes at work. The whole hospital started wearing surgical scrubs so that we wouldn't have to take clothes home that we had worn during the day. At the time we had no idea how this was going to pan out. There was a lot of uncertainty about what we should be doing at home. Some people moved out, some people left London and moved to other parts of the country where they had access to another home. Some were living in other people's flats or staying in a hotel.

One of the hardest things for me was that before Covid-19 we would never have a discussion about whether or not a patient would go to the intensive care unit or not before they became really sick. But we started having to make those decisions as people came through the door, much, much earlier than we would ever have done before. We knew we didn't have the luxury of delaying that decision because we realised quickly that people could come in looking quite well and then deteriorate within hours, to the point that they needed to be put on a ventilator. Everyone did different things across different hospitals, whether those thresholds varied quite a lot, I don't know. You had to make a judgment. And, it was not just the elderly we admitted to intensive care. It was younger people too, those who had a number of other medical problems. In the kidney world we have a high proportion of people who are diabetic and have other cardiac problems. If you've got a finite ability to put people on ICU, and there was data coming out from the ICUs from abroad, suggesting that the mortality was so high, we had to accept that there was a degree of futility in putting certain people into ICU who wouldn't recover. We tried to do it by discussing with the doctors who knew them as patients beforehand, saying, "Look, is this reasonable? Should we be doing more for this person? Should we be doing less? How are they? How have they been before?" We had one or two patients of mine, who got admitted to other hospitals, whose family members told me that the decision was made that they wouldn't get resuscitated. I got in touch with those hospitals to say I think you've got that wrong because that patient was living an independent life beforehand. One person comes to mind. He was in his 40s with Down syndrome, but he had a kidney disease that we had treated very successfully not that long ago. He got admitted to another hospital. His family was told he wouldn't get resuscitated because his exercise capacity wasn't good. I had to have two or three conversations going backwards and forward to the doctors there saying you've got that wrong, we know him and that is not an appropriate response.

There will have been variations in how this happened across the country. I dare say that at the very beginning when things exploded, there may have been some patients who were not offered escalation care, where they might have been had they been in hospital a week or two before it exploded. These decisions are not based on absolutes.

It was very hard to deal with the unknown, and understand how it might affect the nursing and medical staff, your colleagues and friends. The NHS has a huge number of health workers who are from an ethnic minority groups, or originally from abroad. They form the backbone of what we do. As stories were coming out, there was a sign that black and ethnic minority groups were being predominantly affected and there was a real fear that this could go through a huge number of people that we have working with us and that would be a real disaster.

But, there were a few things that were very positive that came out of it. The hospital came together in a way I've never seen before. The medical specialities and surgical specialties had one common goal, which was to figure out how to treat Covid-19 and how to get through this. Medical science can often be quite competitive, but Covid-19 has created a spirit of collaboration like I haven't seen before. I think it's made me appreciate how things can be done.

On my phone are weekly pictures of property bags of the dead, my own death figures captured weekly in a macabre photograph.

Lisa Linpower
Junior doctor.
May 2020

My unlikely but constant companion through this Covid experience has been my phone. By my side, wrapped and sealed in the cellophane bag usually used for little vials of blood on their way from the ward to the lab for testing. It's been my companion throughout, not offering any advice or comfort to me, just witnessing. My phone has seen and heard things it never has before and is unlikely to ever see again, certainly with the relentless frequency that it has done in recent weeks.

In the absence of an NHS mobile phone or tablet on the ward, I've placed it next to an old lady's ear on her pillow, with promises to her daughter that her mum will be able to hear her final words of love as she drifts into unconsciousness, still breathing with shallow, irregular gasps.

Its speaker phone plays the voice of her ten-year-old granddaughter, tearfully telling her grandma that she wants her to come home to read to her again one day soon. Its camera has FaceTimed the lovely man in room ten, his elderly wife and grown-up children, gathered in their living room, faces filling the small pocket-sized screen, grandchildren on more screens within screens who cannot be with their parents because of the lockdown. Thanking him for being such a wonderful dad and granddad, telling him that they love him, and to sleep, now. Its speakers have also played favourite songs, Elvis albums and jazz compilations, songs that families have suggested will provide comfort in those last hours of life. It has been there with me and my patients, who, because of PPE, have never seen my face, to alleviate both of our distress and distract from the sounds of laboured breaths, often remaining in patients' rooms without me, an offering of humanity as I am called to assess someone else.

My phone has been my portal to my colleagues throughout these days, too, whose full faces I rarely see. I am new to this hospital, just a number on the new rota. The hospital now on its emergency Covid rota has been run by WhatsApp groups, the old bleep system, inadequate at the best of times, now almost obsolete. Doctors communicate between teams, shifts and zones, for endocrinology advice from a senior or specialist when sodiums are low, to delirium management. Or when food, kindly cooked by volunteers and community groups, has arrived in the doctors' mess.

On my phone are weekly pictures of property bags of the dead, piled up in the store room waiting for collection by the porters, my own death figures captured weekly in a macabre photograph. Each bag represents a person I cared for, my handwriting in their notes documenting my attempts to save them, and eventually, to keep them comfortable when alive, to be followed by my handwriting on certificates after their death.

The phone's torch light has proved useful for confirming deaths in the absence of pen torches on the ward. The faces of my beautiful smiling children in the forefront of my view on the home screen, merged with the torch reflected in the dead man's eyes before me in real life - pupils fixed and dilated - a visceral reminder of a separate world that I have inhabited over these weeks, associated with an intense pang of guilt that I had, in that moment, somehow exposed my babies to a world I should be protecting them from.

The final role my phone has played during the Covid pandemic has been when I am lying in bed at night, unable to sleep or waking from vivid dreams. My phone distracts me, trailing through social media mindlessly. I try my best to avoid any news. I don't want to be consumed with any bigger picture for fear of being overwhelmed. Able to cope with my micro-level involvement with this pandemic, my phone has allowed me to stay connected and also disconnect. It has been my lifeline.

We are clapped for our bravery and our care. I certainly do not feel brave. I feel guilty for not being able to do more.

Sarah Ryan
Doctor.
May 2020

One of the hardest aspects of the pandemic for me was the difficult conversations with patients and family members. As a hospital doctor the decision about whether CPR and intensive care treatment is appropriate for the individual in front of me is an everyday consideration. Patients and family members are often reluctant to have discussions around this topic and conversations can be difficult and emotional, but Covid infection can cause such rapid deterioration it is even more necessary than usual to have them early.

Furthermore, we had no definitive treatment for the disease and had seen very few people successfully discharged from the intensive care unit. The possibility that every patient may deteriorate to the extent that they required an ICU stay was so much higher than before the pandemic. The patients were scared, the families were scared, and I was scared that they would not survive this illness. Then you start talking about what would happen if their heart was to stop and whether it is appropriate for them to be admitted to ICU. Understandably, this is often too much for people to handle.

These are not conversations we like to have, but they are necessary. The Hippocratic Oath says that we are first to do no harm. Inflicting a treatment on a patient which is very unlikely to be successful goes against this. However, often families and patients felt this was due to lack of resources. It is challenging to explain the futility of these treatments without instilling more fear and distress.

The medicine of Covid is not tiring. I do not have to use my brain to put on an oxygen mask. The numerous challenging conversations were what sapped my energy.

I feel guilty for not being able to do more. We do not know enough or have a cure. I cannot provide reassurance when patients feel like they can't breathe. I cannot tell them we can do this treatment or that treatment to help. I have to turn up the oxygen and stand back and cross my fingers. Then we are clapped for our bravery and our care. I do not feel like I am doing my job properly when I can't change the course of the disease. I certainly do not feel brave.

I tried to focus on the small wins. I was looking after a confused elderly patient with Covid. He wasn't really engaging and couldn't answer questions. He kept chatting about watermelon. We got some watermelon from the corner shop. He took one bite and seemed to snap out of his delirium. He told me about how at home he would get a whole watermelon every week and crack in it half and scoop out the flesh. He wasn't too impressed with the prepackaged stuff we had brought, but it was worth it for that moment of lucidity.

Some of these patients were ventilated for up to 40 days. In this day and age that just doesn't happen, and we had multiple patients like that.

Sarah Gotke
Specialist respiratory physiotherapist.
June 2020

It was all quite strange at the beginning because we were thinking, "What is happening? Why are we doing this? Is it really coming or is this just pretend?" And then the patients started to come through the doors, and I kept thinking, "Oh my god, this is something I hope I never witness again." The reality of it was hard. Staff crying, being exhausted. That is not something we see every day, especially in such a small hospital but with Covid-19 we did.

During the pandemic our intensive care unit tripled in size, and once the pandemic began we had to very quickly adapt and upskill lots of staff to be able to cope and treat the sheer number of patients that were coming in and being ventilated. They were the very sickest of the Covid patients. Staff who perhaps worked in day surgery, who didn't really have anything to do because so many other areas of the hospital had just shut down, helped us care for these patients. We just desperately needed staff, staff and more staff. These people had basic nursing skills and I had to try and upskill them. I had to try and give them some sort of education abotu what it might be like, before we rostered them on to help in intensive care. Lots of people volunteered. We were training every day of the week to give them a flavour of what walking into an intensive care unit would involved. Some of them had never seen anyone on a ventilator before. In six weeks, we trained 170 staff. They got one day's training each, then they were rostered on and thrown into it. Without them there's no way we would have had enough staff to care for these people. It couldn't have functioned as it was. It was an uphill task. Unbelievable. But we did our best. After the training was done, it was all hands on deck and I went back to being a physio on ICU.. I was assessing patients' chests, the energy going into their lungs, and cleaning their lungs. We would try and use a number of different positioning techniques and breathing techniques to help maximise oxygen consumption. Then, if they survived, I would be involved in the weaning process, where you get the patient off a ventilator and breathing on their own again.

On a daily basis, doctors, nurses, speech and language therapists, and physios come up with a plan about what is best for a patient on that particular day. There isn't a set protocol that fits everyone, and Covid patients can be on ventilators for such a long, long time. Many of them are on sedation much heavier than we normally use in ICU, so they were taking a long time to wake up. Everything was just taking a lot longer. The process of weaning them off the ventilator was a lot slower too, and all the time I'm thinking, the longer they're in bed, the more they're likely to have more problems with their strength, and their muscles. Every single day they're in bed and not moving, they are getting weaker. The best thing we can do is get them up and walking and moving as much as possible, as quickly as possible, but that process throughout this was a lot, lot longer and a lot slower than how things usually worked with ICU patients. A lot of these patients were heavily sedated, paralysed and aware of absolutely nothing for weeks sometimes months. This has a massive impact on the patient's recovery longer term. You lose around 4% of your muscle mass every single day you're on a ventilator. It's the same for the respiratory muscles, so it's trying to reduce that decline as much as possible. But obviously, with Covid patients, they had prolonged stays on ventilators so they were losing muscle really, really quickly. From a breathing point of view, it's very hard to teach respiratory muscles to breath for themselves again when a machine has been doing it for so long for them, and some of these patients were ventilated for up to 40 days. In this day and age that just doesn't happen, and having multiple patients like that was astounding. It's because the virus stops the lungs being able to get oxygen in and around the body. Sick, sick patients were needing high levels of oxygen to get it into their blood and circulating around the body. But Covid was causing multi-organ failure, so they weren't able to transport the oxygen across.

Whether patients are suddenly able to breath for themselves again or not seemed to be down to luck and determination. The ones I saw who died, had just given up. They didn't want to survive. They would quite openly tell you, "I'm done. I can't do this anymore." It is really, really hard work for them. It is painful. There is a huge amount of anxiety, confusion, delirium. They are constantly gasping for breath. It is frightening. But we have to tell them just to go with it. They have to push their bodies to give it even a chance of it getting strong again. There is definitely a psychological element to survival. Those that did recover had a real drive to get better. I remember one lady in her mid-60s so clearly. One day, I was treating her and she had started to do brilliantly, but by the afternoon when we went back to see her, she really wasn't doing so great. There had most definitely been a psychological change in her. She had decided she'd been through quite a lot of health issues in her life, and this was just one too many and she wanted to give up. She wanted to give up that fight. For her, it was a choice. She didn't want to continue treatment, and she died. That can be hard, because we could have continued the treatment, but she actually said she didn't want to. She had the capacity to make that decision. She wasn't confused. She was very clear about what she wanted and the path that she wanted to take. She spoke to her family and explained why she had made the decision to give up, and it was amazing. She had a dignified death and it was what she wanted.

We had one gentleman. He was unbelievably sick. I remember working on the Saturday and everything was against him. He came in with a lot of renal issues around the kidneys. Over a couple of weeks, he just deteriorated and then ended up coming up to the intensive care unit. They tried CPR (cardiopulmonary resuscitation) and non-invasive ventilation, but it just didn't work. His oxygen requirements went through the roof. There was nothing more that we could do so we ventilated him. Even then, things were just not getting any better. His heart was giving up. He was experiencing multi-organ failure. I remember standing in a corridor with a consultant and he said to me, "I think his time is up, we have tried everything." I came in on the Monday, not expecting him to be there for a minute, but he was. Whether his body just decided, you know what, I'm not ready to give up yet, I don't know. He is a total and utter miracle. I do not know how he managed it. I now see him every week doing my rehabilitation sessions. I look at him all the time and I think, "I cannot believe you're still alive. You had everything against you." The possibility of survival, even when all hope had gone, was always there. You just never ever knew with Covid, but you can never ever care for a patient thinking it is a waste of time. You can't. You have to hold on to the hope that there's a chance they might get through this. That person could be your granddad, your dad, your son. If you were nursing them thinking that this was a total lost cause, then you just wouldn't be doing your job. There is a percentage of people who really should have died, but they didn't. They survived and will go on to live the rest of their life for a very long time.

I was never worried about getting it myself. You didn't have time to think about yourself. You just got on with it. You did your job. You were there to serve the patients and try and help them get through this. That's just what we do. If it was one of my family, I would want people to go all out & do everything to help them, so I'm happy to do that for somebody else's relative. That's what I signed up for. Either join the Covid battle or not. You're there to care for the patients and hopefully get them better to get them home and live the rest of their life. If you can't put your hand on your heart and say that you were happy to do that, you shouldn't be there. You never know when you might be in that situation. For me, there was no question. I go into work. That's what I do every day. I've done it for the last 20 years, and the reward is amazing. Yes, there are some sad days and low days, but the reward is huge. That's what motivates me. Seeing people get better, seeing them improve, seeing them be able to call their grandchild or see their wife again. That's amazing. I am lucky. I get to see a patient's whole journey from the beginning, potentially to the end with their rehabilitation. I get to see them back at home. I get to see them getting stronger. I get to see them get their lives back. They consider us one of their friends.

We just don't know how long term they will suffer yet though. They are going to have lung function issues. Some of them are still very breathless, even doing minimal activity, and that has a huge impact on how they can function on a daily basis and if they will ever go back to work again.

That has a huge psychological impact, and the journey is only just beginning for some of them. Another huge problem is that they don't remember a lot about their experience. Some of them are only facing the news and the press about it all now. They're having to process the fact that they were one of those victims, and the reality of coming to terms with that is going to be a real problem long term. It is a very unique situation to be faced with, the fact that you simply do not know what happened to you during a period of your life. They have no idea what happened to them when they were ventilated. We had one guy who missed his birthday. He's never going to get that time back. He's never going to have that birthday again. Some people can deal with that, but others really struggle psychologically with it. You can almost tell the moment they walk through the door whether they have a strong mind to deal with the trauma of their experience or not.

Mental health in this country isn't something that is dealt with well, and we don't have services in place. There's a huge lack of services and a shortage of people who are trained to deal with it. What counsellor is now trained to deal with a Covid patient's mental health? Nobody yet. We don't even know what the long term effects are, let alone how to treat them. How can you empathise or give them ways to cope with something you have no understanding of. You can't possibly know what they've been through, waking up after being sedated for more than a month. Their lives have quite literally passed them by, they've not had any natural light for 40 days and then they open their eyes and see people all dressed up in PPE and think they're aliens. How do you start treating that?

For seven weeks of the pandemic I moved out of the family home and away from my husband and two children, and mother-in-law. That was a choice I decided to make. I owed it to them and to my mother-in-law. If anything happened to her and I gave her the virus, I couldn't live with myself. I got to see my 12 and 14 year old at a distance, but that's all. I didn't hug them for those seven weeks. I didn't eat with them. I didn't kiss them for eight weeks. It was really tough. It was bedtime that I struggled with. Kissing my children at night as they go to sleep is huge. It's part of our family life. I missed that terribly, but they will remember this pandemic for the rest of their life, and they know my job is important to me but they also know that their granny's life is just as important as my life. So to them, it was really important that she was going to be alright and that I stayed away.

Probably in the next six months, I will look back and digest what has happened and be proud. I finish work each day and think, "Have I done the best job possible? Have I made a difference today?" That's basically what it comes down to. That's important to me, and I can honestly say I felt that most days leaving work during Covid, and I still feel that today.

Covid patients didn't look like they were struggling or panicking, despite being so unwell. It was surreal. A silent ward with a silent killer.

Eliana Shekarchi-Khanghahi
Senior house officer. Redeployed to
the Covid High Dependency Unit.
May 2020

I was quite excited about being assigned to a Covid ward. I liked the idea of being in the thick of it, but I had no idea what was to come. I'd get to work, put on my PPE and it felt like I was entering a dehumanised, depersonalised zone. You're so hot. You're so uncomfortable, and we were unidentifiable. We'd have to write our names and roles on our gowns so people knew who we were.

Daytime on a ward felt very different to night-time. At night, there are typically fewer doctors around. It's eerier, and it seemed like the condition of our Coronavirus patients' conditions deteriorated at night. They seemed to get more and more unwell.

One evening, it was me, a registrar and two other junior doctors, and from the moment we started work the machines didn't stop bleeping, the phones didn't stop ringing and the questions just kept on coming. The four of us just went from one patient to the next. They were dying one after the other, falling like dominoes, and the work just never stopped. As the shift wore on, the patients just got sicker and sicker. That was how the virus seemed to work. In the daytime, you'd do the ward round, everyone seemed stable, but at night, it was like a continuous domino effect. Everyone seemed to get unwell, and you were never completely on top of it.

What you did with a Covid patient just became second nature after a couple of shifts. It was like an algorithm in your mind even though it was a completely new disease. We put them all on antibiotics, even though we knew it wasn't bacterial, but you did it to protect them from any infection. Then, there's the need for oxygen. That is what Covid patients always seemed to need most. We would try and "prone" them, which is when you turn the bodies of patients in respiratory distress on their stomachs. On their backs, the lungs are compressed by gravity.

What unsettled me the most was that Covid patients didn't ever seem to look that ill. It was creepy. A silent ward with a silent killer. Patients would just sit there breathing really, really fast with incredibly low oxygen levels. Somebody could be awake and talking to me, and you'd look at their oxygen levels and think, "how are you managing to do that when your levels are so low? How are you even sitting up?". From the end of the bed, you would never think that they were so critically unwell. That's how all the Covid patients behaved. They looked relaxed. They didn't look like they were struggling or panicking, despite being so unwell. It was surreal. As a doctor, I know when someone is really unwell. Things don't look right. It's instinct, but with these patients I'd think, "You're talking to me. You're smiling at me." I would ask them how they were and they would all say "I'm alright, thanks. I'm ok". I'd question them again and again, and they'd insist, "Honestly, I'm okay, I'm okay". Then, two hours later they'd be about to have cardiac arrest, and if you didn't do something, they would die. I would think, "How can you go from that to that, so quickly?". It is like no other illness I've ever experienced. This virus does exactly as it pleases. It feels like a monster takes over a patient's body, and you feel helpless.

Our team was amazing throughout the worst of it, and so wonderful at morale boosting. The consultants were baking about five cakes a day. There was warm apple cake for breakfast, a massive banana bread late in the morning, but there have been really testing times.

When I was asked what skills I could offer in this pandemic, I immediately thought of my palliative care skills. I used to work in a hospice, in end of life care, which I think helped me deal with it all. I know how to make death as dignified as possible for patients, and I did.

One night, when we went on the ward round, we knew that one man was dying, and I just stayed with him and held his hand. I've never done that before. I've never sat with someone when they've taken their last breath. His watch kept on ticking and his phone still got texts as he took his last breath. I watched as someone, who'd had a long, fulfilling life physically left this world, and I shed a tear.

I rang his brother to tell him that he'd passed away and explain to him that I had treated him as if he was genuinely one of my family. That's what all of us have been doing, because their own families can't be with them. I know that gave his brother so much comfort but you almost get embarrassed because then they start thanking you. You feel awkward because you don't want anyone to focus on you. That makes you even more emotional.

His brother sent me a card at the hospital which was very, very emotional. I was having a horrible day and had just done three night shifts and someone told me a card had been delivered for me, and I just broke down. I just couldn't understand how he did it, why he did it, surely it was the last thing on his mind. I just thought, "if I've done anything in my career of value, that is the most important thing that I've done so far".

I've never been scared for myself during this pandemic, only my parents. After my first crazy night shift, I just rang them and said, "Please stay in. Don't go outside. I've seen some terrible things and I don't want you to be exposed to this in any way, shape, or form, and I mean that."

My boyfriend is also a doctor, and he works in Intensive Care. He rang his parents and told them the brutal truth too. It would frustrate us both seeing people not following social distancing. If you could see what I've seen, trust me, you'd be following the rules. I chose to be a part of it though. It's a part of our history and you want to be able to help, and know that you did something to contribute. I actually looked forward to going into work because the rest of the world felt like it had stopped.

I've also never felt closer to people at work. They were like my family. Even on my days off, I found myself wanting to be with them all again. They get it. We were in this bubble together. The first time I heard the Clap for Carers I was sitting having a beer at home, and I started to cry. I thought, "this is amazing". It wasn't because it was anything to do with me, but because I thought, "everyone is in this together". All I wanted to do was shout, "I love you all. Are you all okay?"

I think I feel more proud of my job than I ever have. I can't imagine doing anything else, but I have witnessed an absolutely horrible virus that wipes people out in a way that I've never seen before. We lost really young people. We lost colleagues. There are staff still in intensive care, so all of our best qualities have had to come to the fore to be there for each other. When you go through something traumatic or emotional with a group of people you have a strong bond. I don't want to leave that, and I'm optimistic that it might change everyone's view on the NHS. I've been a doctor for five years and I've never seen people come together like this. I've never worked in such an amazing, supported environment in my life.

I've woken in the night convinced I'm on a ventilator. I go to bed anxious. I wake up anxious. I cry at the simplest offer of kindness.

Paul Bolton
Lead nurse for infection prevention & control.
May 2020

I'm sitting in my car. The engine is running to recharge the battery as I wait for my wife to come out of the shop. It's a Saturday and I've just finished work absorbing and interpreting the latest update to advice on PPE, arranging for patients to be correctly placed, arranging testing for staff and providing general support and advice across the Trust.

Recharge. It's something I tell my team to do at the end of every day. You've done your best. Go home and be with your family. Recharge. Trouble is I'm not sure how to do it myself anymore. I came home on Thursday this week empty. Not an ounce of energy left to talk or be nice, be dad, a husband, anything. All I could manage was to sit mute and then try to sleep. I've run ultra marathons, I've trained hard for Ironman events and helped to bring up two children. This is a whole new tiredness I've never felt before.

I think I'm also grieving. I'm grieving for all that has changed. For missing friends, family and colleagues. Planned futures and dreams. I'm sad for my children and all that they are not able to do, and for my wife, for all that she has given up to try to be a mum, wife, teacher and counsellor to all of us.

I've gone through the disbelief stage: the denial of this impacting on us the way it has with admissions, deaths, running out of beds, equipment, drugs and basic equipment to use. Disbelief has slowly shifted to the next issue that I was sure we would not be affected by. Each one has slowly but steadily arisen and become accepted as fact. This is what we do now. This is what we will do from now on. A critical care unit tripled in size. More than 40 patients and staff were being tested every day. Trust guidance changing to reflect the ever-growing impact of this virus on our population.

I'm lucky in the job I do. I still have one to go to every day. I haven't had any of the emotional exposure colleagues have from seeing friends admitted to hospital. But, emotionally I'm worn out and I'm beginning to shift from disbelief to anger. Anger we are in this situation. I need to be sure that this does not affect my role but that is hard to achieve in a high pressure environment.

I miss time to be silly and unwind. I miss long quiet runs where nothing scarier than "am I lost?" interrupts my thoughts. I know that there are many people in much worse situations, I know that I should be grateful for health, family, a stable job... but aren't we always told what we feel is what we feel? That how you are affected by a situation is very different to anyone else. I look to colleagues who are much stronger than I am, or at least appear to be, and wonder how they do it, when I am struggling.

I'm tired of interpreting various non Public Health England guidance and separating fact from fiction, evidence from opinion. Looking at pictures of PPE from other countries and defending why we are not doing the same. With this comes the absorption of everyone's anxiety and upset: a full time job in its own right. We have been doing this since January 2020.

In three months we are, in my opinion, no nearer an end than we were when we started. We are just at the beginning of what will become a new normal. Some of this is positive. There was always a need for more critical care beds, more nurses, more respect for what the NHS delivers. We were always doing amazing things, with less money, less interest, less praise and fewer beds. But these positives seem small beans compared to the toll I see this taking.

I've held onto too many thoughts. I've woken in the night convinced I'm on a ventilator. This is a common dream amongst all critical care nurses I think, and many of us have told each other what we do and don't want to be done if we were ever admitted. I go to bed anxious. I wake up anxious. I cry at the simplest offer of kindness. I feel drowned by the depth of emotion that floods me each time I stop to think.

I stood outside the room where the Covid patient had just left and I thought, "Oh my god, this is it."

Paul Hicks
Cleaner.
July 2020

I am 61 and I've been working as a cleaner at Poole Hospital for 20 years. I'm responsible for deep cleaning every room where a Covid patient has been treated. It's my job to decontaminate it and make it safer for staff and patients. We have to wash everything from the ceilings to the walls, from the floors to the equipment. From the very beginning of the pandemic, I've been unfazed by the task. I'm not frightened by it. It's just hard graft. We work our socks off, and very few people are willing to do it. I feel proud to do a job I am good at. I can make a difference in that hospital. I'm making it safer and that gives me a great sense of achievement.

Since the pandemic started I've actually increased my hours, so I suppose I'm actually putting myself in more danger now by working more, but I can see the results of the effort I put in. Staff say, "Wow, look at that. It looks lovely," and I feel proud that I can make the nurses happy after I've been in and cleaned. But I can't lie, the very first time I went in to clean after our first Covid patient left, I was anxious. I stood outside the room and I thought, "Oh my god, this is it." I put my visor on, and my mask and my hat and long gown, scrubs and gloves and went in. There are just so many things I have to remember now, so many different bags for things to go into, so many different procedures I have to follow, and it is so hot and sweaty, and much more difficult to move around, and the masks are so tight on my face. It was so daunting, but I genuinely enjoyed it. I never want to let anyone down.

I do worry about my wife and my family getting it from me though, so I religiously change my clothes as soon as I finish work, put my uniform in a polythene bag, keep it separate from everything else. When I get home, I don't let anyone else put it in the washing machine. I leave my work shoes at the hospital and clean everything before I go into the house. The only way I can get through these times, is by being silly and making people laugh. I have to tell jokes to make it less stressful, or I take in biscuits for patients and staff. They deserve more than digestives, so I take in custard creams! My Mum always taught us to be kind to people. That's all I'm doing. We didn't have much when I grew up, but we were happy and we supported each other. I just try to do that and not stress about things. It is my job to do things for other people so the clap for the NHS was always very special and emotional for me. It felt good. I liked the recognition but I wasn't comfortable with it either because I am proud to do my job whether it's during a pandemic or not.

We have to put their bodies through torture to keep them alive. It is invasive and agonising, but some do get through it. The human body is incredible.

Kirstie Hill
Intensive care nurse.
May 2020

When I went into work I felt like I was in a completely different world. I entered the building differently, I had to dress differently, behave differently. It was suffocating. Patients were disorientated, they didn't make any sense, they were scared. It was shocking, and I am someone who is used to intensive care patients. One night, my partner asked me what it was like and all I could say was that it must be like walking on the moon. It felt so alien. It was really unsettling.

Thinking back now, I probably didn't cope with it as well as I should have. Not at all. I've suffered with PTSD (post traumatic stress disorder) in the past, so I am fully aware of my own mental health and how to manage it, but other people I was working with were experiencing a massive professional change, doing a unfamiliar job in a unit they'd never worked on before. They didn't know me or how I operated and I didn't know them. Add to that, the fact that nobody had any alone time, or any chance for headspace, or escape. We were either at work or with our families, trapped at home. It was intense. Cycling was my way of dealing with the stress. When I was on my bike, I would think about nothing else but pedalling. That was my way of coping with it. You feel free on a bike. It's just you against the elements. As nurses, we see so many people in worse situations than our own, so it's very easy for us to put aside our own emotions, and not address them. We just take it on the chin and carry on. Being a nurse is not just my job. It is who I am as an individual, but there was definitely a point when I had to say, I need to take a step back from this, I'm struggling. It was the constant stream of people, the absolute relentlessness of it, the inability to escape from it that was so hard. Every single day you just didn't know what situation would confront you when you walked in the door, what kind of patient would be there, who would have died. There were so many patients losing their lives day after day. It had a massive impact on me.

For the entirety of a shift, I would have one patient to look after exclusively and that patient was mine. I wanted to go to the extreme for them. I would always start my day by introducing myself to my patient. You just never knew if they could hear you. I'd tell them what date it was, what day of the week it was, what I'd been doing since I left work the night before. I'd brush their teeth, make sure they were clean and their dignity was maintained and then work from top to bottom with the drugs they needed, making sure that they were pain free, that their heart rate didn't go too low, their airways stayed clear. I'd watch for any signs of distress, any abnormal heart rate, monitor the pressure levels, check their kidneys. You are constantly thinking of the next thing that needs doing whilst keeping an eye on what is actually going on at that moment. I would go for hours without a drink or a toilet break because you can't leave. The other nurses have their patients to watch over. It takes too long to take all the PPE off and put it on again. Your brain is constantly whirring.

People die and that's life, but some moments have been more awful than others. One of my patients was a Dad in his early 40s, and one day I'd spent 10 hours of my shift with him, doing everything I could to keep him alive, and I mean everything. He needed multiple organ support. I was administering medications that could kill him if I didn't do it properly, and nothing was working. He was just getting worse and worse and worse. I had to call his wife and his children for them to say goodbye to him, and on another phone I had the chaplain who was saying prayers for him. Meanwhile, I am still throwing every treatment I can at him and it's just not working. I was sweating in places I didn't know I could sweat, my head was banging with such an incredible overload of information in my brain. I felt like I could no longer keep up, and then I was told not to do it anymore, to admit defeat. That just destroys you.

What's also been so hard with Covid is not knowing anything about who we are looking after. Normally, in intensive care, we have face to face interaction with the families, they come in for visits and that's how we find out about our patients, or we get to know them before they deteriorate and end up in ICU. With Covid, I had to try and think outside the box. I'd ring a patient's family on my way home and try and find out what music they liked, what they did for a job, what their favourite food was so that I could talk to the patient the next day about it, even if they were unconscious. You just never know what they might respond to. I have done this job for nine years. It's probably what I was always meant to do. It might sound strange but I enjoy my job and I enjoy intensive care and I enjoy looking after sick people. Every nurse will tell you that they enjoy it. I am in such a privileged position, but I am only one person, and my brain can only take so much. One of our very first Covid patients was discharged today. He's been with us for a long time. Seeing him leave ICU was just amazing. He has been through so much, and we helped him get there. We have to put their bodies through torture to keep them alive. It is invasive and agonising, but the human body is incredible and some do get

We have all had to work with inadequate protection, going home every night, not knowing if we were going to infect one of our kids.

Anonymous
Consultant chest physician.
April 2020

I had been somewhat dismissive of the whole situation being "just flu" back in January until a WhatsApp chat with some of my old uni friends. We were talking about "herd immunity" and it dawned on me that this was a total fallacy and that by pursuing this strategy we would be permitting the deaths of hundreds of thousands of innocent people. When I saw what was unfolding in Italy, I just knew we were going to end up in the same situation.

And so it came to pass. When we got our first case, a patient from a care home, I realised how dire the situation was. It meant that the virus had been transmitted at least two weeks before by a visitor or a carer who probably got it themselves two weeks before that.

When we were all talking about "just flu", under the misapprehension that this was a Chinese or Italian problem, nothing to do with us Brits, community transmission was already with us. How could we have been so stupid?

We weren't totally overwhelmed in terms of bed but difficult decisions were being made. People you would have given a chance on ITU before Covid no longer had a hope because they had high blood pressure or diabetes or obesity. Just normal people.

We thought ITU would be full, but what we actually struggled with was the number of CPAP machines [a continuous positive airway pressure machine that delivers a steady flow of oxygen to your nose and mouth] and the oxygen supply.

We were given these random home ventilators, not what we had ordered weeks ago, as everything was being centrally procured. When they came, they were not fit for purpose, we had to scrabble around, finding extra oxygen flow meters to make them work. Even though we had extra machines, we didn't have enough oxygen to use them all. Our estates team had put in a bid to boost our supply but all the engineers were at the London Nightingale hospital. There was nothing we could do except wait and make do.

Don't even get me started on PPE. It became obvious that guidance was changed according to supply. What utter bullshit. To think I went along with it, trying to "enforce" this on our ward. I feel complicit, but at the same time, we have all had to work with inadequate protection, going home every evening, not knowing if I was going to infect one of my young kids or my husband with his high blood pressure and metallic heart valve.

It was easier to push these thoughts to the back of my mind and pretend they didn't exist, but the stress was there. I was a bitch to live with, because of the sheer pressure. Shouting at the kids, snapping at my husband. I felt important, that I was doing vital work, but all I wanted to do was go home and do the kids' schoolwork with them. I missed them so much.

In a way the medicine was the easy part. We couldn't do anything. We just held patients' hands and hoped they would get better, both of us feeling helpless. Yet every step was a struggle, getting the right equipment, the right staff, the oxygen. The disconnect between what was happening on the wards every day and "Gold" command and beyond.

I don't take the free meals we get given, I would rather they went to the patients or people who have no money as they can't work. And now the lull, before, perhaps, a second wave. I have time to think about what just happened, how I would do it differently given another chance, and about those we couldn't help.

This is not the beginning of the end. This is a lovely end to the beginning. This is not going away.

Zudin Puthucheary
Intensive care consultant.
May 2020

We always tell our junior doctors that if something goes wrong in intensive care, there should be no reason for the consultant to put down their cup of tea. They should have prepared for every eventuality, and we spent a lot of time at the hospital early in the year doing just that. We were preparing and preparing and preparing, even though we didn't really know what we were preparing for and nothing was actually happening. We were exhausted before the pandemic even really hit, but we could see what was happening in China and in Italy. It then came to us and it was surreal.

I was working on the first weekend when the pandemic really hit. It was scary. One of our patients turned out to be an intensive care nurse from another hospital. She was a colleague, and she had been watching all these people around her slowly deteriorate. The same things were happening over and over again. People would come in on a bit of oxygen, then they would need more, then they would be put on ventilators. It was just a relentless progression and nothing we seemed to do seemed to change that. That night, I had to sit there and tell her that I was going to have to do to her what I'd had to do to others on the unit, and put her on a ventilator. She was begging me not to. She kept saying, "But look at all these people, I don't want to be like them." This was one of our colleagues. She had been watching this for 24 hours. You can imagine her fear, her panic. She knew she'd be going through what they had gone through. It is brutal what we have to do to the body when we intubate (insert a tube into the trachea for ventilation) someone. I had to explain to her that if I waited then it could be even more dangerous. We did intubate her in the end. She did survive. Just. But, she'll be horrifically disabled for quite a while, because she was ill for a very long time, and the longer you are ventilated the more your muscle wastes away. You lose about three to four percent of your muscle mass every day when you are critically ill like this.

The other element to this pandemic that we are unused to, is the fact that almost every single intensive care consultant I work with got ill too. My wife found that very hard, because she's not used to me ever being ill. I am a fit and healthy 40-year-old but I was getting chest pains that were waking me up at night and that was scary. What also struck me was how the pandemic was perceived by different ethnic communities. Those views made our jobs so much more difficult. Our hospital is located within a big Asian community near Whitechapel in London, where many believe that coronavirus is a government conspiracy to try and kill people. This belief isn't helped by the data that shows if you are from the BAME community you are more likely to suffer with Covid. It means that the community you are working within is immediately suspicious of everything you do. I am Malaysian, therefore Asian, but as far as many of the families I dealt with were concerned, I was part of the hospital therefore I worked for the government. We were dealing with a lot of mistrust and distress from families. We can normally get around these concerns because they come into the hospital, they see how we work so understand that we are sincere in what we do for patients. That just wasn't possible with Covid. They never met us. We only had conversations with them on the phone. That is no way to build a rapport, so they didn't trust us. It was soul destroying.

While I worked in London, I had to leave my family in lockdown in Northamptonshire every day. I have two young children, one is just five months old, so it has been incredibly difficult for my wife through all of this, but I needed to go to work. It's not a job, it's a vocation. I look after people who are in no state to look after themselves in a very, very complex setting. It is my job to provide clear direction for the team to keep people alive.

There aren't that many intensive care consultants around, and we can make a huge difference to people's lives. That is why I go to work. If I am not there, life will be worse for the patients.

We have been dealing with the unknown and as a medic and an academic researching this pandemic, there has been a genuine tingle of excitement too, but what has frightened me is that our politicians don't understand what we do, yet they have been the ones deciding how to deal with the infrastructure. More deaths will result because we will be hamstrung. The MPs clap for the nurses but they don't pay them enough so they can pay their mortgages. There is a real belief that no one really cares about them.

I will look back on this time and feel proud. We are all proud but we are broken, and the second wave will come. It's not a case of if but when, and I think professionally it will crucify the nurses. They are exhausted. So much has been demanded of them and they have been incredible. I am used to death, as much as anyone can be, but understanding death during Covid has been so difficult. We've really struggled. I got to a point where I didn't want to call family members anymore because every time I arranged to chat to someone about the progress their relative was making, they got worse. People could be completely stable for two days, maybe three days and then become very, very unstable very, very quickly. Patients have had to watch other patients die alongside them. There are no longer curtains between patients because we need that space for more beds. That's psychologically destructive for a sick patient.

And, I haven't been able to turn my brain off since this began, so I worry that if I switch off, I'm not sure how easy I will switch it back on again.

Covid is everywhere. It's conditioning how we live, it's conditioning what's on television, it's probably conditioning what we dream about.

Susan Michie
Professor of behavioural psychology, and member of the Scientific Advisory Group for Emergencies (SAGE).
May 2020

I was asked to join the Behavioural Science Advisory Committee for SAGE, which generates a huge amount of additional work. There's attending meetings, but there's also contributing to briefing papers, in some cases leading on briefing papers that then go to SAGE, often with very tight deadlines. You might have three days in order to produce a new policy paper.

One I led on was considering different options for increasing adherence to lockdown. I get probably 300 emails every day, or something like that. That stacks up, it's an additional huge amount of work and creates anxiety about getting behind in your day job. I'm also doing a lot of media work, so I probably have at least two or three media engagements a day, going on television, radio, and speaking with journalists. I've never worked so hard in my life.

I feel very motivated, because, obviously, the problem is huge and there's a huge amount to do. So many health psychologists want to get involved and to do their bit in terms of Covid. We've got people doing new surveys, we've got people doing rapid reviews, I've brought people in to help with research projects. So many want to apply their expertise to Covid because it's so preoccupying: it's everywhere. It's conditioning how we live, it's conditioning what's on television, it's probably conditioning what we dream about. The academic community has been amazing in the way that they've really rolled up their sleeves and got stuck in.

What's also clear is that the public has been amazing too. If you think back to when this began in Wuhan and China went into lockdown there was a narrative that we would never do that here. That we were a liberal democracy and that you could never expect the British public to put up with that. But we have and I think this shows we mustn't make assumptions about people.

This has shown that people are essentially kind, sensible and intelligent and if you give them the information, in this case about the severity of the situation and about how what is expected of them will help save lives, then they will respond.

The assumption by some politicians that people won't do things or can't understand things has been proven very wrong. We are adaptive creatures and we wouldn't be here today if we weren't. I think the population has shown themselves to be outstanding, especially those who are living in really challenging situations, with overcrowding, no outside space and massive anxiety about money. This has shown we have the inherent ability to make sacrifices for the sake of a common good and show a generosity of spirit and collective solidarity.

I'm 64 and I'm missing my three children and grandchildren. They all live within a couple of miles of me and a really important part of my life, and not being able to see them is distressing. It's emotionally challenging. But it's emotionally challenging for everyone.

We are a small team Ben Machell, Lucy Watson, Laura Whateley, Matt Curtis, Matt Nicholson & Nathalie Lees. We have donated our skills as writers, editors, illustrators, designers and developers and self funded this print run to give NHS staff a platform for their voices to be recorded. All profits from the sale will go to NHS Charities Together. For a digital version of this book go to <u>frontline.site</u>

Thank you Robert Crampton for writing the foreword, to James Griffin for giving us his new typeface Castling and to Clays for generously discounting the print of this book.

Thank you to our NHS.

Copyright © 2021. All rights reserved.
No part of this book may be reproduced in any form or by any electronic or mechanical means, including information storage and retrieval systems, without permission in writing from the publisher.